DREAMS
ARE BUILT OVERNIGHT
HOW TO CREATE A BRIDGE BETWEEN YOUR DAY JOB AND YOUR DAYDREAM

TO: Nia,
Your non-profit will effect more people than you think. If you DON'T build it, They won't be effected! "DREAM BIG"

FROM:

DAVID SHANDS
FORE WORD BY: DR. ERIC THOMAS
SLEEPLESS SOCIETY PUBLISHING CO.

Copyright © 2015 by David Shands.

Edited by Monica Goings, Vice President of Sleepless Society Publishing Co.

All rights reserved. No part of this publication may be reproduced, distributed or transmitted in any form or by any means, including photocopying, recording, or other electronic or mechanical methods, without the prior written permission of the author, except in the case of brief quotations embodied in critical reviews and certain other noncommercial uses permitted by copyright law.

Ordering Information:
Special discounts are available on quantity purchases by corporations, associations, and others. For details, contact:

dreamsarebuiltovernight@gmail.com
www.dreamsarebuiltovernight.com

www.sleepis4suckers.com
All social media: @sleepis4suckers

Booking Information:
To Book David Shands for your next speaking engagement, please contact:

david@sleepis4suckers.com

1st ed.
ISBN 978-0-692-56565-0 (print)

DEDICATION

I dedicate this book to **you**, the dreamer. **You** have both a job and a dream, and **you're** working around the clock constantly building a bridge between the two. **You** work at **your** job all day but build **your** dream all night.

You know who **you** are.

You know that an hour of **your** time is way more valuable than the hourly wage that they put on **your** paycheck. **You** sit in class and **your** teacher has no idea how brilliant **you** are because she's inaccurately judging **your** brilliance based off poor test scores.

I wrote this for the child of destiny.

Harriet Tubman freed herself from slavery, but she came back to show others how to do what she did for herself. I left the plantation, but I came back with a road map for **YOU**.

Table of Contents

Foreword 9

Chapter 1: An Introduction to Yourself 13

Chapter 2: Overslept 23

Chapter 3: The Day I Woke Up 31

Chapter 4: What If Your Passion Won't Pay You? 35

Chapter 5: "Why?" Life's Most Important Question 43

Chapter 6: "How?" Take the First Step 51

Chapter 7: "But I Don't Have Time" 57

Chapter 8: Do What You Do, Don't Become What You Do . 63

Chapter 9: Product of Your Environment 69

Chapter 10: $100 Off-Days 77

Chapter 11: Free Lunch 83

Chapter 12: Outgrow Your Business 91

Chapter 13: Grab Your Paintbrush 97

Chapter 14: Sacrifice: How Much Will Money Cost You? .. 105

Chapter 15: Pray About It 111

Chapter 16: Blind Faith 117

Chapter 17: Conclusion 125

Chapter 18: A Letter to Mom 131

Chapter 19: I Need to Call Dad 139

Bonus Chapter: School is Just a Game 147

sleep

/slēp/ 🔊

noun

1. a condition of body or mind in which one is highly unproductive and accepts average living conditions.
2. a mindset possessed by those who believe what they believe solely because they've been taught to believe it.

verb

1. being inactive, dormant or enjoying excessive amounts of leisure while still having a list of outstanding unaccomplished goals.

verb: **sleep**; 3rd person present: **sleeps**; past tense: **slept**; past participle: **slept**; gerund or present participle: **sleeping**

Sleep is 4 Suckers

Dreams Are Built Overnight
-David Shands

There is something to be said about someone who teaches based on personal experience as opposed to theoretical lessons on the topic of success. I often come across very ambitious, articulate, charismatic, motivational speakers and authors who teach the principles of success by using information they have learned from successful people. By using your God-given charisma, attending Toastmasters meetings, having the ability to properly structure a presentation, and branding yourself as an expert; motivational speaking is a fairly easy industry to be involved in—so much so that it's trendy right now to be a speaker and "life coach." I find it comical, however, that most of the speakers I come across who want to teach about success aren't successful themselves; even by their own standards and definition of the word—for instance, the authors and blog writers who write about how to have a successful relationship but are not married, or the speakers who can articulate 5 steps to living a happy life but still work at a job that makes them unhappy. I can't wrap my mind around the fact that professors can find a job teaching business courses at a university without ever actually owning or operating a business themselves! But in this case, David decided to write a book about how to transition from your job to your dream because he's actually done it! I cannot cosign a book written from the perspective of theory; I can only cosign successful application, and I've personally watched David effectively make the transition from his job to his dream.

    A few years ago, I was in downtown Atlanta having dinner with David for the very first time in person. He was energetic and hungry to get more out of life, and the fact that he was very humble and respectful is why I decided to promote his brand on my web series without asking for anything in return. What I enjoyed most about our conversation is that not once did he mention anything about hating his job as a server or wishing he didn't have to go to work in the morning. He appeared to be very content with what God had blessed him with up until that point, but he still had a very passionate ambition to achieve more. That is what I would consider the formula for a happy life: ambitious content. He told me how God had blessed him with a very flexible job that allowed him to build his business and make money simultaneously. He said that the restaurant industry allowed him to pick up shifts if he needed money, or give away his shifts to other coworkers if he had an event to attend for his business.

As I listened to his story, I felt the need to stretch him a bit. I felt that if he let this go on long enough, his comfort would rock him to sleep if he wasn't careful. I didn't mean to rain on his parade, but I just had to tell him straight up, "I don't know how you'll feel about it, but you're going to have to quit your job." The look on his face went from excitement to pure bewilderment. I recommended the book *Outliers* by Malcolm Gladwell, and I explained to him one of the most critical principles of the book. I told him that one of the chapters talks about the 10,000 hours it takes of doing something consistently to master it. This principle holds true in my life as well as the lives of countless others who have achieved excellence in their respective fields. I calculated the hours of speaking it took me to become one of the top 5 speakers in the world, and it came out to having done it for over 10,000 hours! I told him, "David, trust me. Every hour you spend at that job that you like so much takes away from your 10,000 hours." I could tell that he wasn't prepared to hear this information at the time, but what he did with it drastically separates him from the crowd—he actually QUIT! People all around the world revere me as an expert on becoming successful. I've become economically valuable because of my ability to share principles and insights on how to create a lifestyle that most people only dream of. I understand the psychology behind poverty and how to break the cycle of generational poverty. I speak to millions of people worldwide, but only a very small percentage of them will actually apply the information and implement it immediately. When I got the call that David put in his 2-week notice at the Cheesecake Factory, I knew this kid was a different breed.

    I recommend this book to anyone who has a dream—anyone who has a desire to be more than what their job title says they are. The very simple yet powerful and practical principles in this book can help anyone, and I mean anyone, make the transition from their day job to their daydream. These simple tips can be applied by a waitress, bus driver, school teacher, corner office executive, or stay-at-home mom who wants to build something special. There are people waiting for a job that only YOU can provide. Stop being selfish by staying at your job, and go out and create something for others to enjoy.

— Dr. Eric Thomas

CHAPTER ONE

An Introduction to Yourself

Dreams Are Built Overnight
-David Shands

Buzz… *Buzz*… *Buzz*… the all-too-familiar sound of that beyond-annoying alarm clock abruptly breaks the peace of Wayne's slumber as he rolls over and routinely begs his alarm clock for 10 more minutes of peace by smashing the snooze button. It's now 6:40 a.m., and the buzz strikes Wayne's eardrums again with a mighty blow that startles him. Wayne quickly counters with a haymaker to silence the sound as he obeys the alarm clock's final demands to wake up and get dressed for another day of "8th grade incarceration" (or so he calls it). Wiping the sleep crumbs from the corners of his eyes, he slowly resurrects from his pillow-top tomb and reaches for the nightstand lamp in order to create light in a Godlike manner. After a few minutes of having the swag of a Michael Jackson "Thriller" zombie, Wayne searches in his closet for something he hasn't already worn this week, lays it on the bed, grabs one of his three pairs of sneakers that he feels best complement his outfit, slides them at the foot of the pair of jeans that are draped off the side of the mattress, and heads to the bathroom to get dressed. Fifteen minutes later, Wayne is off to the races.

Fifteen YEARS later, Wayne is following this SAME routine of eardrum strikes, snooze button counterpunches, and outfit layouts at 7 a.m. However, he is used to it by now since he has been doing it since grade school. The only difference is that instead of a book bag, Wayne grabs his suitcase; instead of Reeboks, he grabs his Rockports; and instead of trash talking on the bus with friends, it's traffic and talk radio on his morning commute.

The mass majority of America has a schedule that looks like this: wake up, go to work, come home, go to sleep...wake up, go to work, come home, go to sleep...wake up, go to work, come home, go to sleep. WAKE UP...GO TO WORK...COME HOME...GO TO SLEEP...day in and day out...5 days per week... 40 YEARS straight! Even if the job changes, we generally fulfill our 40- to 50-year obligation of "the cycle" until we either can't physically work any longer or we die. But I cannot help but think that over a 40-year period of helping someone else build their dream, you had to have at least thought about how fulfilling it would be to build your own. You've HAD to daydream once or twice about being in control of the 24 hours of your day and not just 16, leaving the remaining 8 hours to the hands of someone who tells you what to do, how to think, when to eat, when to use the restroom, how to treat their customers, what time you have to be where they tell you to be, and what time you are allowed to leave. To some extent, they control your days off as well. For instance, if you want to go visit your mother in Tennessee and you live in Georgia, your job determines the earliest you can get there and how long you can stay. So over 40 years of missing your kids' games and recitals, cutting vacations short, getting side-eyed for taking sick days, and getting looked over for promotions, the thought of taking your life into your own hands has certainly crossed your mind, I am sure.

Naturally, the next thought that crosses your mind is: "But how? Where do I begin? I have a job that is very demanding, leaving me very little time to pursue my dream. I have a girlfriend or spouse who demands that we have date night on Sundays, which shaves a day off my weekend and shaves $50–$75 each week off my bank balance. I have kids who need my time and attention. My car has been acting up lately. My best friend just broke up with her boyfriend and she needs me right now, and blah blah blah, excuse #329, and more blah blah blah stuff!"

An ex-girlfriend of mine told me one time (well, actually, all of them have said this to me at least once), "You make time for what is important to you." For example, what if someone told you to attend a class EVERY DAY, from 10 p.m. to midnight, 7 days a week, for 6 months? You would probably say that you are too busy to fit something else into your schedule, right? But what if they said that at the end of the class, if you didn't miss a day and you were never late, they would give you 2 million dollars cash? How many excuses would you come up with about why you could not make the class then? I would be willing to bet that you wouldn't come up with any excuses as to why you couldn't make it. If anything, you would probably shift that excuse list from the class and hand it to someone else who wants some of your time: "Hey babe, I have this class I have to go to tonight; we might have to reschedule."

There are two main reasons you probably would not make any excuses and would do whatever you had to do to attend this class. For one, you deem this activity important. You are willing to trade your time and effort for an activity that will give you a return on your investment. Secondly, you have a specific date as to when it will pay off. There is a finish line that you can actually see. In this scenario, you are aware that 6 months from today, if you do everything you're supposed to do, you are going to get the 2 million dollars that was promised to you upon completion of the class. You can be EXHAUSTED from a race, drained beyond measure; but when you get close to the end and can actually see the finish line, you'll find the strength to run even harder and even faster when you are coming down the stretch. There is something about your eyes seeing the goal that escalates your desire to have it, and everything else decreases in importance. Have you ever had to use the bathroom really bad on your way home? You're in the car and it's very uncomfortable, but the moment you get out of your car and put the key in the door, the uncomfortable feeling magnifies dramatically! You can't get that key in the door fast enough! That feeling gets even worse when you get to the bathroom and try to undress. There's just something about us humans that when we can see the finish line and we know that we're close to the end, everything intensifies. We find our hidden energy and second wind. You would be early to every class if you knew the date that it would pay off. The only problem with entrepreneurship is that you have no idea when the payoff date will arrive.

  Moving toward a destination that we cannot immediately see can be very disheartening, frustrating, nerve-racking, and requires faith to keep from being fearful. I was driving to Huntsville, Alabama, from Atlanta, Georgia, and I found myself low on gas. Shortly after I realized that I needed to fill up, I noticed a gas station on the opposite side of the road. Now for some reason, I HATE stopping at gas stations that are not on the same side of the road that I'm driving on, especially if there is a median that makes me have to pass the station and go backward. Instead of looping around, getting gas, and getting back on track, I decided to wait until I saw another gas station that was easy to pull into (I know that's lazy, but I was lazy when I was 19). I drove for about 3 miles and didn't see any gas stations. At this point I'm not panicking, but I'm starting to get a slight feeling of anxiety in my belly. Another couple of miles go by, and I start getting frustrated. I drive another few miles, and now I am officially nervous! All I could think about was how lazy and dumb I am for not stopping at the gas station that I saw several miles back.

    I now have two options: I can either keep driving with the faith that a gas station will pop up soon and I won't be stuck on this country road in my 1986 Toyota Corolla that doesn't have air conditioning to begin with, or I can turn around and go back to the place where I definitely knew a gas station was located. However, now I run the risk of running out of gas to drive another 5 miles back in the opposite direction. After weighing my options, I decided to go back to the place I knew for a fact had gas, and I barely made it. The funny thing is, on my way back as I pass the point where I originally turned around, I realize that if I had kept going, the next gas station was about a 30-second drive up the street!

    I tell that story to say this: if you are unsure about where you're going, it's hard to stay the course. This experience also taught me that the fear of moving forward into the unknown will make turning around look like the most logical option. If a baby is being abused by its mother, when Child Protective Services comes to save the child, the child will generally cry to go back to the very mother who abused it. As humans, we would rather have a KNOWN abuse than to walk into an UNKNOWN situation. You may be relieved to know that faith is not the absence of fear; in my opinion, faith means you move forward in spite of fear. It's not that superheroes are not afraid of their enemy; it's just that they fight them while being afraid. A brave man is not a brave man because he's not afraid—he is brave because he handles his business afraid. Do it afraid! Every time I do a speaking event, I am somewhat nervous. I am afraid that I may say "umm" too many times, or afraid that I may misread my crowd, or afraid that I may encounter a heckler; but I just DO IT AFRAID! I have faith that God gave me a message that I am supposed to spread, and this is what I have been called to do. That's why we as humans would have no problem attending the 2 million dollar class and being consistent in showing up—because we know that the finish line or reward is coming at a designated time. However, it is a bit harder to pursue your goals if you don't know if your success is coming in 6 months or 6 years.

This journey toward success can be extremely discouraging, but I believe that success is a formula. It is an equation that takes people a lifetime to solve, and in most cases they go to the grave never finding the answers. I think I am getting closer and closer to cracking the code. It is one thing to become successful; you could have gotten lucky or tapped into your own special gifts or talents that won't transfer past yourself. However, it is another thing to be able to create success—to give someone else the formula, and it works for that person as well. This is when you will know you have cracked the code: not only does the combination unlock your success, but someone else can use that same combination and unlock their own.

Because of my limited interest in academics as a child, I never really understood the complicated scholastic subjects, so I needed information spoon-fed to me. Had I been more engaged at school, I wouldn't have such a handicap in digesting BIG information today as an adult. However, because of this handicap, even in this book, my writings are simple. Not many big words, but very practical information. The information I offer is from a very simple place because my range of understanding is simplistic and narrow, and I am very surface and practical when it comes to business. Some people are so smart, so complex, and so DEEP that the simple answer, which is generally the real answer, is never good enough because it is too simple to them. Less intelligent people just need to be smart enough to hire more intelligent people to solve the problems that they can't. I have never, ever been the smartest guy in the bunch, but I have always been smart enough to know that experience is the best teacher. If you read and researched everything about how to swim—every technique, plus how the water and your body communicate—you still would not fully understand how to swim until you jump in. My whole life, I've been willing to skip the research-and-development part and just jump in the pool. My body began to communicate with the water naturally. What I know to be true is that if you spend enough time in a pool, eventually you'll figure out what to do. I'm not telling you to not do your research, because I've bumped my head a bunch of times by failing to investigate, but I'm used to the pain by now. I guess it's what they would call both a gift and a curse, my ambition and ignorance. I call it ignorant ambition.

Most everyone I know who has a job also has a dream. The question is: how do we bridge the gap between the two? Thanks to social media, thousands of people have been able to witness my transition, but Instagram, Twitter, and Facebook did not tell the whole story. What I can say about this journey is that it wasn't easy, but it was very simple. Simple, meaning that anyone can do what I've done, which you'll see as you continue to read. I'm just a regular guy, who had a regular job, who came from a regular family, with regular circumstances. No money, no investors, and no connections. No celebrity friends, no special training, and very little education. This book will help so many people because I didn't skip any steps due to favorable circumstances. I know some people who, about a year into their business, found an investor by the grace of God. Or, out of the millions of people who auditioned on Shark Tank (including myself), got on the show and made a powerful connection with an industry titan. I know some people who already had really good relationships with sports figures and celebrities, so they got an instant cosign. Now, I'm not saying that anything is wrong with getting in the game by any of these avenues. And I'm not saying that these people didn't strategically orchestrate these connections and make themselves available to receive these opportunities; I'm just saying that I didn't. I'm just like YOU. The only advantage I had was the chance to watch my mother struggle to provide for my brother and me, and that put the battery in my back. My fear of not being able to provide her with the life she deserves was greater than my fear of failure, so failure was something I was willing to face head-on until I got things right. Let's begin.

CHAPTER TWO

Dreams Are Built Overnight
-David Shands

After an exhausting week of classroom-style training, today is my first day of training on the floor. For the next few days, all of us will be shadowing experienced servers as they teach us newbies the Cheesecake Factory way. I'm excited to have gotten this job because my money is looking real funny at this point. I have been looking for a job and applying to every restaurant in the city for the last few weeks since being fired from my last serving job. Ironically, I got fired from the Olive Garden for stealing a slice of cheesecake and serving it to my mother without ringing it up and putting it on her bill... and now I find myself a server at the Cheesecake Factory (go figure). Today I'm shadowing Kat. There could not have been a better person for me to be working with for my first day of on-the-job training. She was super cool, easy to work with, and very knowledgeable about the CCF system. After asking all the important questions, like "How much money can I make in tips?", "Which managers are cool, and which ones should I avoid?", or "How can I get the good sections?", we began to get to know each other on a personal level. She told me that she was an aspiring singer (she actually sang me a song that day, and her voice was amazing—simply angelic). As the shift went by, we talked about a wide range of topics including music, politics, and relationships. We got as personal as two strangers can get before they decide whether or not they like each other. I asked her how long she had been working at the restaurant, and she replied, "About 3 years now."

"Really—3 years?" I asked (as if I didn't hear her clearly the first time). "That's a long time!"

She said, "Yeah, it kinda flew by."

My silent thought to myself was, "Wow, 3 years? Ain't noooo way in the world I'm gonna be here for 3 years! Serving food, refilling drinks, dealing with babies, smiling through the ignorance of certain guests who look at you as a 'food bringer,' and living off tips for 3 years...not gonna happen! I'm not trying to stereotype, but being able to look at a certain guest and be 95% sure that I'm about to get a $5 tip no matter how much the bill was, for 3 years? No way...NOT ME!" I knew for a fact that for me, this job was simply a means to an end.

Fast-forward to about 3 weeks later. I find myself running a few minutes late for my morning shift. Walking through the door as fast as my "coolness" will allow, I fall right into staff alignment as my general manager is making announcements. Staff alignment is a 5-minute pre-shift meeting where management gathers everyone together to go over the commitment for the day, inform us of any changes to the menu, give us somewhat of a motivational pep talk, and update the team about any staff birthdays or anniversaries. During this particular staff alignment, my man Jimmy (the absolute coolest general manager who ever walked the face of this earth; Jimmy made working for the company an enjoyable experience and really made people feel as if they were part of a winning team) walked up to me and announced that I had been working for the company for 3 YEARS! I stood arrested in silence for about 10 seconds as he handed me my "3 year" pin.

"Why are you giving me this pin?" I questioned. "You must be mistaken, Jimmy—I think this is for someone else. I've only been here for 3 weeks!"

He said, "No no no, son, you've been here for 3 years! I checked the records this morning."

"Are you sure?" I pleaded. "I could have sworn that I started about 3 weeks ago!"

With a slight grin, Jimmy placed his hand on my shoulder and said, "No, David, it only seems like 3 weeks! Time flies when you're having fun."

Snapping out of this daydream scenario, I regained consciousness, took my 3-year pin and said, "Thank you." I actually ended up working for the company for a grand total of 6 years before I finally quit.

How did this happen? How did 3 years feel like 3 weeks? How did I start working a job with no intention of being there longer than a year and end up spending a total of 6 years in the same position? Around the same time, I found a guy who was worse off than me, and luckily I had a conversation with this gentleman before it was too late. I was at Ryan's Buffet on a Sunday evening for a family get-together, and I ran into an older Caucasian man as we waited in line for some hot, fresh dinner rolls to come out (for anyone who lives in the South and has been to Ryan's, you know that those rolls are not a game and are well worth the wait). I'm not sure exactly how we began talking, as this was years ago, but I remember that we began to chat about our families we were there with. I quickly discovered that he recently retired from his job, and I asked him how it felt to not have to go to work in the morning. He said, "It takes some getting used to. I worked every day for the last 45 years at the same job, and it takes time to break out of a 45-year routine and get used to figuring out what to do every day."

I said, "Wow, 45 years at the same job—you must have liked working there since you stuck around for so long."

He said, "You would think so, huh? But it didn't really click with me that I was there so long until about two years before I actually retired. Time just kinda flew by, ya know?"

At this point, I was really intrigued with his story since I'd never met anyone who actually retired from a job working 40+ years straight at the same place. I said, "Time just flew by? What do you mean?"

He said, "Well son, if you're not careful, your daily routines will rock you to sleep, and when you wake up your beard will be as gray as mine. I worked the same job, with the same hours, doing the same thing, every single day for 45 years. I knew what my schedule was, I knew how long I would be there, and I began to plan my life after 6 p.m. or on the weekends. I knew what I could and couldn't pay for, so I adjusted my life around my responsibilities. The first few years, I was figuring out how to do my job, the next few years I figured out how to be just as productive with less effort, and the last 30 years I coasted. I could do my job with my eyes closed after a while, and I felt true job security."

"Didn't you get bored, though?" I asked.

He said, "Sometimes, but every time I got bored or felt like I wanted to do something else, they gave me another small raise." He chuckled with a loud old-person chuckle, which was accompanied by a little cough as if that laugh took a lot out of him, which ultimately made me laugh with him. I'm in awe of this conversation because for a split second I saw myself as him. It was like a 3-second nightmare as I envisioned telling some young buck how I fell into a routine, 40 years from now. He said, "I do regret it though, because outside of work I only remember a few significant events in my life. One was the day I got married to my beautiful bride, who is sitting over there waiting for me to bring her another dinner roll. The second was when my daughter was born. My boss let me take a whole week off from work to spend with my wife and new baby girl. Do you know what the next significant event was, young man?"

I said, "Ummm, watching your daughter take her first steps, or hearing her say your name?"

He said with a sigh, "If only I were that lucky. The next significant event I remember is when my daughter's daughter was born. My boss let me take another whole week off from work to spend time with my granddaughter." My heart dropped into my sneakers as I listened to this story being told by a man who can't buy his time back. "I just fell into a work routine and scheduled my life around that. If I could do it all over, I would figure out how to make money from my house. Even if I only made just enough to shelter and feed my family, I would do it, but I got comfortable at work because the job was so easy to me and the money was enough."

The server came and switched out the empty pan of dinner rolls, replacing them with a fresh, hot batch. By this time, I had forgotten why I was even in line. The older gentleman looked at the fresh rolls with a slight grin, took two off the pan, and with a slightly shaky hand placed them carefully on his plate. He said, "It's not as bad as you think though, because now I appreciate how precious my grandkids are, and I spend every moment I can with them. It was nice talking to you, son. Enjoy your dinner." As he walked away, it felt like my feet wouldn't move as I commanded them to. This was one of the most significant conversations of my life, and at that moment I realized that for the past few years, my routine had rocked me to sleep. And at that point, I'd overslept.

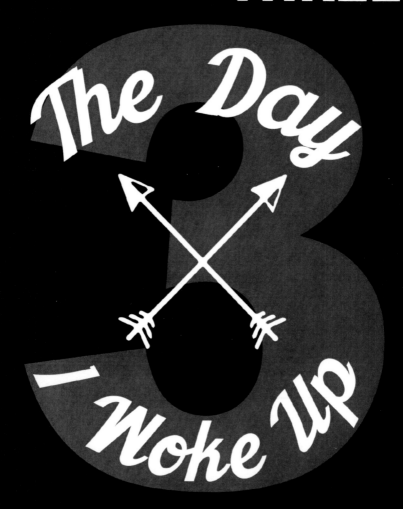

It's a Friday evening shift, and I'm having a very good night. The tips are flowing; the guests, with the exception of 1 or 2 (there are ALWAYS 1 or 2), are in great spirits; and my food is coming out of the kitchen flawlessly! My favorite managers are running the floor, I have a green ticket in my pocket (which is what employees use to order a complimentary meal after their shift), and I am not in a closing section, so I will be the first cut from the floor. At this point, life is good! I find myself cutting bread for my last table of the night, and my friend walks up to me and casually asks, "What are you doing for your birthday this year?"

I think for a second and say, "I don't know—I haven't thought about it."

She says, "Well, let's go back to Club T&G like we did last year for your birthday. I know we can get everyone who works here to come out this year like they did last year. We can even put some money together to get a bottle for your birthday!"

I say, "Aight, that's cool—just let everyone know." She agrees and walks off. Suddenly, in the very moment when she walks away excited, a feeling of disgust falls over me. I felt like I was in one of those movies where everything surrounding me went dim and quiet, and it was just me and this loaf of bread in my hand.

If you had been a bystander, you would have overheard a conversation between two coworkers talking about future birthday plans, but I heard a conversation between me and myself discussing past that I heard went something more like this:

"David, do you realize that you're celebrating your birthday at the same place and with the same people you celebrated it with last year? Not that anything is wrong with that, but think about it: you work at the SAME job, you drive the SAME car, and you live in the SAME place you did last year. Your bank balance hasn't changed much in the last 12 months, and you know you're going to have to buy a new birthday outfit since your closet looks about the SAME as it did a year ago. You have been equally productive this past year as someone lying in a coma for 12 months. What has changed about you in the last 365 days other than your age, David? Nothing? Okay, I was just checking."

I had another one of those "heart in my sneaker" moments, and I realized that it's no coincidence that I keep getting these revelations. Have you ever asked God for a sign, and He sends you one, but then you ask for another one because that one didn't really make you feel the way you thought a sign should make you feel? Then you ask for another sign, and it's even clearer than the last one. I felt as though God was wasting His "signs" on me, and He'd eventually stop sending them since I'm obviously not accepting them. I have a few mentors who give me advice, but if I never use the advice that I ask them to give me, I'm pretty sure they'll stop answering my questions. Hypothetical question: does God ever stop speaking to you if it's obvious that you're not listening? I ask myself weird, out-of-the-box questions all the time, and this is one that I didn't want to find out the answer to. We all have these moments when we get fed up with our current circumstances. We know that God has called us to something greater than what we're currently involved in, but for some reason we don't move. It all really comes down to disobedience. If you tell your children to clean their rooms and they don't, that's called disobedience. Even if they do it, but they don't do it until next week, it's still disobedience because they didn't do what you asked them to do, when you asked them to do it. I feel like I was being called to affect the world and help people walk into their God-given purpose. I feel that I was being called to motivate, inspire, and educate the next generation. God gave me a gift of being able to connect with the youth in a very unique way, but I wasn't doing it... disobedience. I got sick of being disobedient to my Heavenly Father, so now it was time to work. But after I hear a motivational speaker, read some inspirational books, and finally make a decision to change my life—after the adrenaline settles, the question is: "What do I do now?"

CHAPTER FOUR

Dreams Are Built Overnight
-David Shands

People will tell you all the time that if you pursue your passion, you will reach your goal. This is not necessarily true and is not a very good strategy for success, in my humble opinion. Wise words from one of the most successful investors in history, Mr. Warren Buffet, said "Whatever YOU like to do, make it a hobby, and whatever the WORLD likes to do, make it a business." Sometimes following your passion professionally may, in many ways, prevent you from reaching your goal. What do you mean, David? Well, passion is simply a feeling or an emotion. The dictionary describes passion as "a strong and barely controllable emotion." I have learned over the years as an entrepreneur that following my emotions has been very bad for business. I try not to make emotional decisions at home or at work because they generally end up badly. High emotion disrupts clear thinking, and unfortunately I had to learn this principle the hard way more than once. If we are defining passion as a strong uncontrollable emotion, and emotions are defined as a strong agitation of "feelings;" if I told you to pursue your passion, I would be telling you to follow your feelings, and THAT, my friend, would be the worst advice anyone could give another human being. If the couple who has been married for 50 years followed their feelings, I'm sure they would have never reached their 50th anniversary, because "feelings" change. If I just went to bed every time I didn't "feel" like working on my brand after getting home from my job, I would still be a server at the Cheesecake Factory. Feelings change but goals don't, unless your "feelings" about a goal change. If you don't "feel" as if you will achieve your goal in a reasonable amount of time, generally you will be inclined to change your goal to something easier to reach. It's not that you don't still want to achieve the goal that you originally set, but your "feelings" altered your course. Here's a good phrase to highlight in this book: "Never stop doing something just because you don't 'feel' like doing it anymore." Before you quit your job, or quit on your relationship, or quit working out at the gym, find a few reasons that have nothing to do with your feelings. Most people who quit their job to pursue full-time entrepreneurship do so because they don't "feel" like going to work anymore. When I quit my job, it was a calculated decision. I loved going to work, but it began to interfere with my business. I didn't make an emotional decision when I chose to resign—it was a well-thought-out, emotionless moment for me.

Your GOAL may be to make music and tour around the country, and that may be your goal because music is your PASSION, which makes perfect sense—I get it. I encourage new entrepreneurs to "count the cost." You look at your goals list and tally up a budget for what you would need to get started making music and touring the country, and the number, for example, is $50,000. If your goal is to travel the country promoting your music, and you need $50,000 to get it done, following your PASSION (which is making music) may or may not be the most effective way to reach your goal. The bottom line is that you need to save up some money one way or another, and if you can get your hands on 50K, you can reach that goal. Now, let's think: is it more important to do what you are passionate about—to reach your goal no matter how little the pay because of how much you love to do it—or would you rather do something that you are not necessarily "passionate" about that may make more financial sense, giving you the capital more quickly so you can fund your GOAL? Allow me to explain.

I was driving through Mississippi on a hot summer day, and I saw something so extraordinary that I had to pull over. I saw a sign that said, "60 socks for $10!" This was so crazy to me that I had to at least see whether it was for real. I had a hard time wrapping my mind around the fact that someone could afford to sell socks for less than $.17 each; I HAD to check it out. Now, mind you, the socks were not the best quality, but at $10 for 60 socks, I would wear two pairs in the winter if I had to. I wasn't in need of socks at the moment, so I passed on the deal; however, an entrepreneur's mind never stops. Some people would drive by the same sign I saw and think, "Hmmm, that's a really good deal. I could really use some socks right now." Others, like myself, would pass that sign and think, "Hmmm, I know some people who could probably use some socks right now. That sounds like a great business opportunity." Now, let's put our thinking caps on. If you bought those 60 socks (30 pairs) for $10 and sold them for $1/pair, you would be turning $10 into $30 and making a $20 profit on your investment. Let's say you invested $50 into buying 300 socks (150 pairs) and sold them all at $1/pair. You just made a $100 profit ($150 minus your original investment of $50). You now have $150 in your pocket, but more importantly, you now have a business! What you may or may not know is that in business, the more you buy, the cheaper the price per item becomes in most transactions. You may be able to go back to the same vendor who sold you 60 socks for $10 and tell him that this time, you have $100 to buy socks instead of $10. Now, this time you can negotiate and say, "Well, instead of 600 socks for $100 (meaning you're paying about $.17 per sock), let's do a deal for 800 socks for $100 (meaning you're now paying less than $.13 per sock)," thereby driving your cost down and pushing your profit margin up! You are now turning $100 into $400 (800 socks or 400 pairs being sold at $1 per pair) by filling a need at an amazing price for your customers. And just that simple, you have now become a capitalist.

Before you know it, what will end up happening naturally is that you'll begin to understand the sock industry. You slowly (or quickly) begin to cut out the middleman. They have great websites like Alibaba.com, which have THOUSANDS of suppliers all over the world who produce, from scratch, products such as…SOCKS! This is when you begin to get better quality at a cheaper price and jump into different colors and more styles, with various cuts and fabrics. You now know what you're looking for. The market (your customers) will tell you what you need and what you don't need. They'll tell you if your socks are too thin or too thick, too high or too low, too loose or too tight. You can have a designer design the socks just how you like them and send the design over to a manufacturer who makes them how you want them. These days, you can build a Word-Press website yourself by watching online tutorials and give people a chance to buy your socks from all around the world! As you expand your product line, you may find yourself attending trade shows with your uniquely created socks, sell them wholesale to stores and boutiques around the country, and continue to build your brand. Eventually you are making enough money for an investor to buy into your company to help you expand and grow your business.

By now, you are profiting and paying yourself enough to save $50,000, which means...YOU CAN NOW TOUR THE COUNTRY SELLING AND PERFORMING YOUR MUSIC (I know you thought I forgot about your passion)! You are obviously not "passionate" about socks, but sometimes you have to be smart enough to figure out how to pursue your passion without starving your family.

I need you to never forget the most significant part about this chapter, which is the fact that all of this began from a $10 investment. I haven't told you anything that isn't practical. I didn't mention your business plan, I didn't mention that you needed a mentor, and I intentionally failed to mention that you need to live in a certain state or must have celebrity endorsements. I did, however, mention that all you needed was the $10 to take advantage of the opportunity. All I did with my T-shirt brand was go on craigslist and find a person who could print my shirts. I asked them how much it would be to print a small run, and their answer was $300. I went to work at my job, saved up a few bucks, and went to work. No business structure, no team—heck, I didn't even have my logo trademarked until about 6 months after I began...I just BEGAN!

In my case, my passion is education, inspiration, and entrepreneurship. My ultimate goal is to build entrepreneurship colleges for children and young adults all around the world, but following my passion meant that I had to build a business that would allow me to get next to kids. I had to do something cool that, when I walk into a high school, I'm not just someone who is trying to motivate them on career day by saying, "You can do it." On the contrary, when I walk in with a Sleep is 4 Suckers shirt, they love the idea and the design; however, what they love most is that I am the owner of the business. I understand that kids love fashion and money. If I can show them how to make money in a fashionable way and also communicate it in a way they can understand, they are all ears—and all I really need is their ears.

Even though I have a successful clothing brand, I am not necessarily passionate about fashion or clothing. I am, however, passionate about learning and teaching. Through the process of building my company, I am learning about business, balance, leadership, and how to manage disappointment. All these topics I teach with great joy! I've found a great way to pursue my passion, without expecting my passion to pay me. Here's the part that you really need to pay attention to: as of late, I have been getting paid to teach (teaching is my passion) the principles that I have learned (learning is my passion) from building a clothing brand (not my passion per se, but it's my business). Sometimes a good business idea and an insane work ethic can open doors to your life's goals, but don't expect the business to always be directly related to what you are passionate about or what you enjoy doing.

I have found out over the years that people do not want to hear from successful people about how successful they are unless they are talking about how they BECAME successful and we, the audience, can also learn how to become that through hearing their story. I feel as though a lot of motivational speakers try to get over by simply trying to motivate people to be successful, telling us that we have the ability to be successful, that all we have to do is think success and write some affirmations on our bedroom walls, and then success will be right around the corner. Now, as much as I believe in the power of positive thinking and writing affirmations, I don't believe motivation will change your life. Inspiration can spark change, but it cannot create change. I believe life change begins with education and action, so I began to walk on a journey of personal development.

CHAPTER FIVE

Life's Most
Important Question

Dreams Are Built Overnight
-David Shands

Most people have a job that they work 40+ hours per week and, at the same time, harbor a dream that they think about just as often. The biggest question is how to bridge the gap between what you have and what you want—between who you are and who you aspire to be—in order to fill the void that has been eating at you for so long. Do you remember when you first got your job? You prayed to God that He would provide for all your needs, and when you got the call for the interview, your excitement was overwhelming! You wore your best outfit and got your hair done for the interview, and when you got offered the position, you were the first person to give your testimony and praise report at church that week. Your first day on the job was exciting, wasn't it? You got a chance to meet some very interesting people, and you set your eyes on being a great employee and possibly moving up in the company. Do you remember how you couldn't wait for that first paycheck to hit your account? And when it did, it may have been even more than you expected. You paid some bills, took care of some stuff, and treated yourself to something you wanted. You had a real sense of moving forward in your life, and you praised God for answering your prayers. God is good, isn't He?

Then 6 months later...an evil spirit of frustration overcomes your entire body every time you think about that place. You have a drink after every shift. You dislike all the managers and half of your coworkers. It's not even that you really like the other half, but you dislike them less than the rest of them. It's like being in jail—you don't really want to become best friends with your co-inmates, but if you are going to be in jail, you might as well make the best of it and have someone to talk and complain to. The money isn't enough, and you're working too hard for the little bit of money they pay you.

Why do we hate our jobs so much? My best guess is that we all have voids inside of us that, if they go unfulfilled, we're not truly happy. I have friends who work in retail who hate their jobs, and I also know people in high power positions who hate their jobs. I know people who quit their jobs because they only made minimum wage, and they feel that the time spent on the job could be better spent doing something that makes them happy. I also personally know people who walked away from six-figure incomes to fill a void in their lives. I met an older gentleman at the airport who has made MILLIONS and MILLIONS of dollars in his life. He began to tell me stories of how he's made millions and how he has also lost millions in business. He doesn't have a financial care in the world. He has a loving family that loves him back, and he's still happily married. He had just sold one of his companies for millions, and he was looking for another business to invest in. He demanded that we sit together on the plane, and the more he talked, the more fascinated I became with the conversation. You can imagine the look on my face when he told me that he wasn't happy. In my mind I'm thinking, "I could see if he had a bunch of money but no family to share it with. That would be a sad scenario to encounter. I could also understand if he had loved ones but didn't have money to do what he wanted to do when he wanted to do it. That too, is a sad situation to be in. This guy has both money and love. There must be a void somewhere." Not to go too far into our private conversation, but with somewhat of a sigh he said, "You know, David, I just want to have fun again."

What is your void? Identifying the void and filling the void are two very difficult tasks, and THAT is why you're never happy at any job you work, no matter how much they pay you or how little you have to work for it. Something needs to be done regularly to fill that void. This led me to the question of "why" Once the question of "why" is answered, this will direct you to that void. The pressing question for most people is: "What do I do first?" when in actuality the most important question is: "WHY am I doing what I'm doing?" I believe the foundation behind ANY successful endeavor is the "why." Asking myself "why" instead of "what" has been a HUGE factor in every decision I make, not just in business. Sometimes asking yourself "why" you are about to do something gives you an opportunity to hear out loud how stupid your reasoning is for "what" it is you're about to do. Sometimes asking a question as sobering as "why" promotes logical thinking. I was about to take this woman I really didn't like that much on a date, but I knew I had some work to do at the office. I knew "what" I wanted to do, but then I sat in my car and asked myself, "Why am I going to spend $60 on a date with a woman I don't even like instead of being productive and getting some work done?" I had a legitimate answer; I said to myself, "Because I feel like going out, having a good time, and relaxing for a change. I deserve it." So my last question to myself was: "Since I want to go out and have a good time, 'why' would I go out with someone I know I won't have a good time with?" I wound up taking myself to dinner and a movie. I had a great time and spent $50 total! It's funny how a three-letter word can help alter, improve, and guide our decision-making ability.

Allow me to explain a more serious reason as to why "why" is an important question. I have a big problem with the fact that a single parent, for example, can raise 3 children on their own, house them, clothe them, and feed them for at least 17 years, but when those children get older, they can't go back and take care of that one parent. This is very disturbing to me. As I am writing this book, a defining moment just happened in my life. My mother surprised me at one of my entrepreneurship workshops that I hosted in Atlanta. Unfortunately, because the parking lot was full, she parked illegally behind someone because she was just going to run in, say hi, and run out. I told her to stay and that we could just wait for someone to leave, and I would park her car in that person's spot. She agreed to stay, and no more than 10 minutes later someone was leaving the establishment. I ran behind them with my mother's keys and asked if I could have their spot. They agreed, so I went to get into my mom's car. As I put the key in the ignition, the car wouldn't start. I tried it again; it started to make some noise but didn't turn over. After about the 4th time of going through this process, the car FINALLY cut on, but it sputtered and shook really bad. It felt as if the car was going to explode! As I was reversing to back into the spot, I had two thoughts: one, if the car breaks down right now, it's going to block traffic, and then I would have to get someone to help me push it into the parking spot, which would be extremely embarrassing. The second thought was that even if I successfully get into the spot, I pray no one sees me getting out of this old aggedy car. How embarrassing would that be for people who are coming to an entrepreneurship workshop to learn about success from a guy whose car doesn't quite paint the picture of "success"? I finally parked, and before I got out of the car, I was so nervous that someone was going to see me that I was preparing my speech to tell people that I was just moving someone's car for them, even if they didn't ask. As luck would have it, the moment I got out the car, I saw a young lady I knew looking for parking. She rolled down her window with a smile and said, "I was just about to park there!" Before she could even finish her sentence, you can guess what I spit out as loud as "cool" would allow: "I was just moving someone's car for them." I suggested another parking space, she drove off and parked in it, and that right there was a defining moment for me, and here's why: the very car that I am too embarrassed to be seen getting out of is the same car that my mother drives every day. The embarrassment I felt for those few moments of trying to start a faulty car—she endures it every day of her life. My heart broke on that day. She simply does not deserve this. She raised me and never let me go hungry, not even 1 day for 16 years straight, and I can't at least change the kind of car she drives? I got so angry with myself in that moment that I had to try to calm myself down and remember that I had an event to conduct.

This scenario created something in me called a "why." You have to find your own personal "why." Your "why" should be so strong that the very thought of this "why" stirs up emotions inside of you. Your "why" gets you out of bed early on your off-days from your job. Your "why" won't let you sleep. Your "why" should be a part of every decision you make. You "why" is a reminder. Some days I honestly don't feel like getting out of bed, but my mom still drives that car, so I can either sleep in or get up and change her car, but I can't do both. So that is WHY I wake up! That is WHY I'm expanding my brand. That is WHY I have to increase revenues and production each year. So when things get tough (and they ALWAYS do), the only thing that will push you over those hurdles is your "why." I thank God for the financial struggle I have experienced my whole life because I have the great pleasure of restructuring my entire family's financial tree. This is an honor, and that's WHY I take it to the max every day.

Imagine for a moment two buildings 1,000 feet apart. Both buildings stand 1,000 feet tall, and I place a board 2 inches wide on top of the buildings to serve as a thin bridge between the two. Say you have a 2-year-old child, and I ask you to walk across this skinny board from Building A to Building B for $100, realizing that if you fall due to a loss of balance, your child will have to live a life without you. Would you attempt this walk for $100? NO? Why not? Well, what about for $1,000? What about for $10,000? What about for $100,000 cash? Most people wouldn't risk their lives for any amount of money, especially if they have children to raise who need their dad or mom. But what if I told you that Building B was on fire and your baby was sitting on top of it? What if I told you that you had just enough time to run from Building A to Building B, grab your baby, and come back before the entire building would be consumed with fire and collapse? Would you make the trip now? Of course you would. The same thing that you wouldn't do for money, you would do if the reason—the "WHY"—was strong enough. You wouldn't even have to think twice about running across the board because what's on the other side is worth risking your life for. The reason I accomplish bigger and bigger goals each year is because my mother is sitting on top of this burning building. I have to save her before it's too late. I need to make as much as I can, as fast as I can, because if I make millions, but it takes 20 more years, my mother won't be able to enjoy the money that I make as much, so there is a sense of urgency for me right now. I urge you to find out what or who is on your burning building. For some, it may be themselves.

CHAPTER SIX

Dreams Are Built Overnight
-David Shands

The "how" is also a very important component of this equation. Figuring out "how" to become successful is not nearly as important as "why" you need to be successful, but the "how" must be figured out nonetheless. As you embark on this journey of going from your job to your dream, this "how" question will come up over and over again for various reasons.

If you were to ask a motivational speaker, life coach, or any unsuccessful entrepreneur "HOW" to become successful, 80% of them would tell you to find out where your passion lies and do it! They may also be inclined to use some sort of cliché quote like, "If you do what you love, you'll never have to work a day in your life." They may also throw in another cliché quote that they read on Facebook that says, "Find out what work you would do every day for the rest of your life, whether or not you were getting paid to do it, and make it a career." Now, both of those sayings are very cute and have a nice ring to them, but I would like to propose another philosophy. Now, before you bash me for using a quote that one of your mentors shared with you, I am not saying it's bad advice—I would just like to give you some different advice. Not necessarily better, just different. You bought this book to hear my point of view, so let me not cheat you out of that experience.

What I realize by doing business development for small businesses is that we all have these grand ideas that require a lot of work. There are so many steps to take. We get nervous and so confused as to what step to take first that we never take any at all. I was told in the beginning that I should not release my clothing brand until I had the logo trademarked, which is very important. I agree with the fact that the trademark was important, but I didn't have enough money to get the shirts printed AND get the trademark. I could have waited to get the trademark and then waited another month or two to register my business name and set up the bank account. I could have then waited another month or two to save up enough money to reserve the website domain and get it up and running. Any good business major would tell you that before you even do all of that, you should save up enough money to get a business plan professionally executed so you will know exactly what steps to take next, and that you should also go to your local banker and build a relationship. I was also advised that before I did ANYTHING, I should speak with an attorney and an accountant (both of whom charge by the hour) about the things I needed to know to run a business. Man, at that point I was just a server working for tips and living by myself. Ain't nobody got time for that! I just could not wait any longer!

    I had an idea to get some shirts printed, so I paid a designer for the design, paid her for the logo, took the logo and the design to a local print shop I found on craigslist, and got the shirts printed. This whole process took a little over 2 weeks and a few hundred dollars, but I was in business! I eventually sold enough shirts to pay for the trademark of the logo, a $1,300 business plan, a cool website, and all that other stuff. I was told about the possibility of someone stealing my concept since it was not protected, but for some reason I didn't really care. I didn't really concern myself with all the things I didn't have—I was focused on what I did have and how I could make something happen right then! It's very possible to be overly ambitious, and actually I didn't trademark my logo or register my name during the 6 months of selling shirts (stupid, I know). Someone could have very well stolen my logo, stolen my idea, stolen the name, stolen everything, but no one did. For those first 6 months, that idea only crossed my mind once, and I remember encouraging myself by saying, "Well, if someone did steal my stuff, the beauty of creativity is that I can always come up with another good idea. They can steal my brand, but they can't steal my brain," and I continued to build this legally unprotected business. I just took the first step, and I was too young and too dumb to realize the danger in doing so.

I remember speaking with an MBA graduate who was going to help me with some structural business development concepts for the brand. He brought some HUGE business books to my house, along with a few of his other MBA friends, and we talked about strategy from a structural standpoint, supply chain management, and all the other things he learned in his business courses while getting his master's degree in that field. He was both shocked and impressed by how large I built my business with little to no structure. I built the business very sloppily; however, it continued to grow. Before he left, he said something that stuck with me. He said, "People like you are more likely to be successful in business than people like me who went to school and spent THOUSANDS of dollars on the information."

I was a bit confused, so I looked at him like the college dropout that I am and said, "What do you mean, bro?"

He put his book down and said, "In my business classes, they teach us about all the potholes, all the hazards, and all the things we 'shouldn't' do to run a successful business. It's a lot to consider when you decide to open a business, and there are certain steps that need to be taken." He said, "People like you just do stuff. You just start. You're not aware of all the dangers and hazards of starting a business; you just jump out the window. Once you're aware of all the dangers and all the things that can go wrong, like I am, it makes it very difficult to move forward. There are many walls that will prevent a business from growing—you just don't know they exist."

This reminded me of a cartoon from back in the day in which a kid is chasing a butterfly, and all the kid is concerned about is catching the butterfly. The kid sees it in the yard and tries to catch it. The butterfly ends up flying across the street, and the kid chases it. The kid doesn't even look both ways before she crosses the street and nearly gets hit by two cars but stays focused on the butterfly. The little girl is then led into a park where older kids are playing football and almost gets trampled by these aggressive teenagers on the field. The football is thrown in the air, and before the football knocks her out cold, the receiver catches the ball, and almost like a running back, the little girl unconsciously runs through a small gap between the receiver and the player who is trying to tackle him. The little girl is still chasing the butterfly. The butterfly then leads her to a little stream of water, and before she steps in the water and drowns, a turtle happens to pop up, and she unconsciously steps on the turtle's shell and gets to the other side, all while chasing this stupid butterfly! The butterfly then lands, and the little girl captures it. This is a perfect illustration of how I ran through the course of building a business. Sometimes, if you are too aware or too focused on the car that is about to hit you, or the football game you are interrupting, or the water that you may fall in, you will never, ever pursue the butterfly, much less catch it. In my situation, the car has hit me on many occasions because I blindly chased a butterfly across a busy intersection. I have been blindsided by my own ignorance more than anyone I know, but that does not stop me from being a habitual butterfly chaser.

    Now, I am NOT saying that you should not get your stuff in order. I seriously suggest that you get a business plan, trademark your business, and pay an attorney, etc.; but you purchased this book to hear my story, and if I had the chance to start all over and do it the right way, I probably wouldn't. I have learned more in my ignorance than I could express in one book, and I will not apologize for being a man of action. One of my mentors has helped me to think first and act second these days, but ignorance on fire in those early days got the job done for me. Again, I'm not saying to start the way I started; it was not the smartest move on my part, but I was more concerned with creating action than creating a favorable outcome. When you're focused on the outcome, it will undoubtedly harness your activity, but if you focus on your activity and completing tasks, the outcome will take care of itself.

CHAPTER SEVEN

"...but I Don't have Time"
society's favorite excuse

Dreams Are Built Overnight
-David Shands

If we were on Family Feud and Steve Harvey said, "Name a great excuse why people can't get ahead in life," I would bet that the #1 answer would be "not enough time," which is a very valid excuse, in my opinion. In fact, it is very unfortunate that so many people are allotted fewer than 24 hours in a day, and successful people like Oprah and Bill Gates are given MORE than 24 hours in a day. If I ever get a chance to talk to God, I'm going to ask Him why He was so "unfair" with the time distribution. Seeing as how I can't talk to Him on their behalf and get their time allotments adjusted right now, I guess I will just have to help these people with the little bit of time they do have.

Seriously though, my mentor, Mr. Jonathan Green, always tells me, "Everything is math." I wrote that phrase on my vision board, and I tell people that in my coaching sessions. It has become like a law for me. "Everything is math" means that the answer to any problem you will face is just a simple calculation. Your problems are generally due to mismanagement or a miscalculation of numbers. So let's count! If we all have 24 hours in a day, the problem that we are facing isn't the lack of time—it's a mismanagement of numbers. We wake up at 7 a.m., leave the house at 8 a.m., fight through traffic, and arrive at work at 9 a.m. We are generally at work until about 5 p.m., and after talking to our fake work friends on our way out and fighting traffic to get home, it's approximately 6 p.m. Those 11 hours from 7 a.m. to 6 p.m. are already accounted for, and there's little you can do about that other than quitting your job. So for the select few who have 24 hours in a day, you are left with 13 hours to accomplish something significant in your life. I have a very simple yet very serious question for you: the same tasks that you tackle daily with that 13 hours, can you do them all in 12? From the time you get home at 6 p.m. till the time you have to wake up again at 7 a.m.— and between helping your kids with homework, cooking, cleaning, spending time with your spouse, doing laundry, and anything else you deem necessary—if you lost an hour, would your life break down? Yes? Okay, cool, I thought you might say that. Well, what would happen if your boss asked you to put in an extra hour at work every day, and instead of 6 p.m. you got home at 7 p.m., but your boss was going to pay you double for it? Would your life be ruined then? I didn't think so. I go through all that to say this: if you can squeeze an hour out of your extremely busy schedule, that's all it takes! Imagine if every day before you begin any of your chores, you lock yourself in a room for 1 hour and called it "grind time." If from 6 p.m. to 7 p.m. you purposed in your heart to do SOMETHING that contributes to your job's exit strategy, how effective would that be? On the surface, that doesn't seem like enough time to replace your income; but if you think about it, every week you would be putting in 7 hours into YOUR business. That's almost a full workday! What if every Friday your boss said to you, "You've arrived at work today to work on your job, but I'm going to allow you to work on your dream for today's shift." That would be pretty cool, right? But one question pops up in my mind: "Will you work as hard on your dream as you do on your job for those 7 hours?" Sadly, most people won't. But that's a business example, and you probably already know that your time management skills when it comes to business could use some improvement, but remember, I said EVERYTHING is math, so let's keep counting.

When I worked at the Cheesecake Factory, I had this great idea to get a composition notebook for 69 cents and write down every dollar that came into my hands and every dollar that left (including that 69 cents). Every day I would have to write down the amount I made in tips at work, as well as the amount of money I spent on bills, food, clothing, etc. If I went to McDonald's and spent $3.18 on the dollar menu, I wrote it down. If I made $100 at work, I wrote it in the book. If I spent $190 on the Jordan's that came out, it went in the book. I began to look at that book weekly, and I could clearly see why I had no money at the end of the week. When I would ask my mentees to do this, by the end of their week, I could clearly show them where their priorities lay. If you were to look at my book, you could tell I was in a relationship at that time. You could see exactly when I started getting serious about my business because you would see less date money and more investment in my product and necessary equipment. It got to the point where I would be in the store trying on sneakers and realize that at the end of the day, I would have to write down this big chunk of money for these stupid shoes. I would have to face the numbers. I remember looking up at the sales associate at Footlocker and saying, "Never mind, I'm not going to buy the shoes. They fit funny." I started to be embarrassed by the money I spent on frivolous things because I knew I would have to face the numbers!

So since you claim not to have enough time to work on your dream, just for the next 30 days I want you to write down how you spend your day. You woke up at 7 a.m., got dressed at 8 a.m., went to work until noon, looked through your social media timeline while you ate lunch from 12 p.m. to 1 p.m., went back to work from 1 p.m. to 5 p.m., got home at 6 p.m., cooked dinner until 7 p.m., ate until 8 p.m., helped your kid with homework from 8 p.m. to 9 p.m., watched TV from 9 p.m. to midnight, slept until 7 a.m., then so on and so forth. This will give you a snapshot of how you're spending your 24 hours. This will be a very sobering moment for you to find out where all your time goes. Hopefully, you'll find the waste in your schedule, and at that point we can find more time to build your dream.

CHAPTER EIGHT

DO WHAT YOU DO DON'T BECOME WHAT YOU DO

Dreams Are Built Overnight
-David Shands

After work, a bunch of my coworkers from the Cheesecake Factory would all go to a local bar and have a few drinks. I did not go too often, but if I had a good night in tips, I would go hang out. I generally worked in a closing section, meaning I would have to take the last tables, so by the time I got to the bar, everyone would already be there. It wasn't hard to spot our crew, because we would all still be wearing our work uniforms of white pants and a white button-down shirt—8 to 12 people dressed in all white with empty shot glasses and half-drunk Long Island Ice Teas everywhere. EVERY gathering with no exception, I would walk into a conversation about the hardships, silly requests, and ignorant comments we all had to deal with from our tables that night. I promise you, if someone started a reality show about the server industry, its ratings would fly through the roof.

Everyone would chime in with stories of how everyone at the table would "chip in" to tip the server; meaning once we see that pile of cash in the middle of the table, we automatically know it is not going to add up to anywhere near the 20% we are looking for. Or the times when they tip $5 BEFORE they even get the bill are the worst; meaning they have no idea that they are supposed to tip based on the amount of the bill, and $5 is really never enough. These stories were hilarious, and we would laugh and drink all night. Coincidentally, the more we drank, the more we laughed. I really did not see an issue with this until my mindset changed through the building of my little shirt business on the side. One day I asked myself, "Why would we come to work, look forward to getting off work as soon as we get there, and then turn around and talk about work all night after we get off?" I started to notice that even if we did not work that day, if I saw some of my coworkers out and about, they would talk about work. If any of our coworkers had a get-together, inevitably the same conversation would spark up after while. I finally realized the problem.

    Some people do what they do, and others become what they do and never find out who they really are. What you do is very important. Why you do what you do is even more important, but finding out who you are in God's eyes will help guide all of that. Some of my friends cut hair, and some of my friends are barbers. Yes, people who cut hair are considered barbers, but you would not think of them as such if you were to describe them. My close friend Shy is a barber, but he is also a barbershop owner. I look at him as more of a businessman than a barber because when we talk, it's not about cutting hair, it's about business. Think of it this way: if I asked someone to tell me a little bit about you, would most of the conversation be about who you are or about what you do, or are the two so intertwined that it would be hard to make a distinction? I am in the fashion industry. I make T-shirts, hats, pants, etc., and sell them in the retail arena. However, if you ask someone about me, whether they have known me for 10 years or 10 days, very few people would tell you that I am a fashion designer, and very few people would make the conversation about my retail expertise. Most of them would tell you about how I inspire, motivate, and lead. They would tell you about my speaking career or about how a conversation with me made them think in terms of becoming or continuing to be who God called them to be. Very few people would talk about what I do in terms of fashion;

most of them would talk about who I am in terms of purpose. I have finally walked into who I believe God called me to be, which seriously guides what I do.

Here's another example: you may or may not know that the Apostle Paul was a tentmaker by trade. Yes, the guy who killed every Christian he could get his hands on at one point and eventually converted to being a true soldier for Christ; the guy who sat in jail and endured violent abuse for preaching the gospel—yeah, that guy. Even though by trade he was a tentmaker, when speaking about Paul, no one would think of tent-making. But do you think that Paul was unable to create some parallels between those tents and his message? Do you think Paul made tents just to make money? No way, couldn't have! Webster's dictionary defines "tent" as a portable shelter made of cloth, supported by one or more poles and stretched tight by cords or loops attached to pegs driven into the ground. I can just imagine Paul sitting with a client as he put one of these things together. I can hear him tell one of his customers, "See this cloth? It is not much by itself. If I leave it outside on its own, the world will do with it what they will. This cloth will go through a tremendous amount of suffering. It will endure rain, sleet, hail, snow, being run over by chariots, being ripped apart by wild animals, and being taken for granted and treated as worthless. The next time you see this cloth, it will be beaten up so badly that it will be unrecognizable. However, if you take this same cloth and GROUND it with these poles, giving this lonely cloth something to hold on to, something to keep it from blowing in the wind, it will not only keep its shape but will also provide shelter for others. You, my friend, are this cloth, and without something to support you, something to keep you grounded, your life can get beaten up pretty badly. But I would like to tell you about a Man from Galilee who can keep you grounded and safe from destruction."

It's ironic that the more I build my Sleep is 4 Suckers clothing brand, the less people associate me with fashion. Most conversations about David Shands have very little to do with fashion or T-shirt manufacturing. People know me more for the message that I spread, not for the items I offer. These T-shirts I sell are not just T-shirts for sale; these T-shirts are my tents. They are tools I use to help spread my ministry the way I believe Paul did with his tents. What are your tents? Or do you do what you do just for money? What is the first thing that people think of when they think about you? Do they think of the server who works at a restaurant? Do they think of the photographer who just takes pictures? Do they think of a barber who just cuts hair? Do they think of a hustler who is always trying to get over? Do they think of a womanizer? I can tell where your heart is, where your passion lies, and who you are by your conversation. Who you are and what you do are so closely related that it is very easy to become what you do and be branded as such. What would our conversation say about you?

CHAPTER NINE

product of your environment

Dreams Are Built Overnight
-David Shands

What you decide to do is very important, and no one can argue that. How passionately you are willing to do what you do is even more important than whatever you actually set out to do. But at the end of the day, your mindset, the philosophy you develop, and the person you become through the process are of the utmost importance. The person I have become through the process of building a company is far more valuable to me than the financial gain of running a profitable business. I believe that human beings over time can change into a far better life form than they are currently. I believe wholeheartedly in the evolution of man. I believe that we can start as one being and becoming a whole new being over time. Now, being a Christian, I do not buy into the Darwinist philosophy in the sense that man was once a monkey and evolved into a very complex, miraculous life form called a human being; however, I do think Chuck was halfway right. Charles Darwin's theory says that whenever a life form exists in a particular environment long enough, over time it will adapt to fit the conditions of that environment. Charles, you could not have been more accurate! I tell people often that your environment will change YOU before you change IT. I don't care how much of a "leader" you think you are or how much you feel you can't be influenced because of your strong will as an individual—the same rules apply. Have you ever heard a song on the radio that you hated? As soon as you heard it on the radio, you despised it. You heard it in the club and still did not like it. Even when you saw the music video, you thought it was the dumbest song ever. But have you ever caught yourself in the car or at the club singing along with the very song that you said is because that song lingered in my environment long enough.

Growing up in New Jersey, I had no idea what an accent was until I moved to Georgia in 2001. I went to Morrow High School, and throughout the entire school year, my friends from up North and I would talk about how weird the other students' Southern accent was. After the school year, I went back home to Jersey for the summer, and ironically enough, all my friends said I had a Southern accent! What? Wait, I am from Jersey, and only being in the South for 8 months, there is no way I sound like them, especially since I made fun of my Southern friends' slow, ridiculous speech pattern and vocabulary all year long. But in spite of how I felt, everyone I ran into when I went home said I spoke funny. Just by being in that environment long enough, I became part of it and picked up traits from the Southern environment. If you hang around a certain environment long enough, you will involuntarily pick up a few habits, words, etc., from that environment. If you hang around those who gossip long enough, over time you will find yourself gossiping. Hang around a church long enough, even if you do not like church, and you will eventually find yourself quoting scripture or even your pastor. Hang around people who curse long enough, and you will find yourself angry one day and watch how one of those 4-letter words slips out. This confirms the validity of the old saying "Birds of a feather flock together."

As I look back, almost every close friend I had growing up in New Jersey sold drugs at least one time in their life, and I'm no different. I ended up getting ocked up in Alabama from carrying these bad habits to college, and that was the end of my drug-dealing career, but the fact is that I did it. While in college, I was a jobless student who tended to "flock" with other jobless college students. We all got out of class by p.m., and we would drink the same kind of beer that we all liked for the rest of the day. We liked the same type of women and involved ourselves in the same type of activities. Now that I think about it, the 4 people I hung around most were other rappers (yes, I was a rapper), DJs, singers, or producers. We shared many common chords, which is why we flocked together.

We have all heard the phrase, "If you hang out with 4 broke people, you are bound to be the 5th." This statement implies that whatever state the 4 people you hang around the most are in; you will be no different, which I have found to be true. The environment that these 4 people create for you will change you in the way of a chameleon. When I began working at a call center and making about $200 per week, even though my 4 closest friends didn't work where I worked, they all had jobs making right around what I was making. When I worked as a server, most of my friends I hung out with on a daily basis made about what I was making. Some a little more and some a little less, but no one in my circle was homeless, yet no one made over 40K. Look at your closest friends, and not just the ones you love the most—I'm talking about the ones you hang out with the most. I would bet that in the majority of cases, you don't make too much more or too much less than your 4 closest friends. But here's the good news: this phrase implies something that is not being said. The phrase "If you hang around 4 broke people, you're bound to be the 5th," implies that all you change your environment by hanging around 4 people who are where you want to be. If I had to attribute my life change to one major factor, it would be my drastic change of environment. I began to understand this principle, sought out everyone I could who made over six figures, and befriended them. The moment I found out the validity of our original phrase, I took inventory of my closest associations and distanced myself. Not that I loved my friends any less, but I had to find out for myself if the edited statement would hold true as well, and I had to start small in order to see how powerful this whole "law of environment" idea was. I found out that the conversations I was having with my 4 broke friends were drastically different from the conversations I had with my more successful acquaintances. It was the craziest thing! In successful environments, if I carried on a conversation about a TV show or a video game that was coming out, they looked at me like I had two heads—as if I didn't belong in that environment. But if I started talking about business or reaching my goals, the conversation would go on for hours. In my "comfortable" environment, if I started talking about achieving a big dream, they would look at me like I was crazy, or at best they would join in for a while, but the conversation would eventually find its way back to television or our club plans for the weekend.

Did you know that almost 80% of inmates in prison go right back in for a different offense within 5 years after being released? The reason this is happening is because the environment of the inmate never changes. David is in the streets selling drugs, stealing and fighting. David goes to jail with the same people who sell drugs, steal, and fight. These people manage to sell drugs IN JAIL and steal from the few personal items other inmates have, and violence obviously isn't a stranger to those hostile environments. Incarceration and neighborhoods across the country apply the same principles, meaning these inmates transfer the same mindset whether in jail or on the block because of the exact same environment. What would happen if prisons created an environment of personal growth and self-development? What would happen if they had mandatory bible study or religious classes that the inmates had to sit in for 12 hours per day? What would happen if they forced these inmates to learn basic academics and morality training for 12 hours per day? What if when someone goes to prison, it is a non-stop course in forced learning? Even if inmates were initially uninterested, after 10 years of hearing positive information and self-development ALL day, there is no way that an environment like that wouldn't breed better citizens! I think our system knows this, but since jails are a big business, they are banking on the inmates to be loyal customers and to revisit their resort as soon as possible. I am sorry—I just veered off into another book that I will probably write soon, but back to the subject at hand.

One of the biggest goals in my life at that time was to make six figures. I wanted to make $100,000 per year because at the time, that was as big as I could dream at age 25. $8,333.33 per month was the goal, and if I was to do that, based on the original principle in this chapter, I had to hang around people who made that type of income. I started to study and follow successful people and paid attention to their language. I even began to create that environment in my house. I would come home from work and watch YouTube videos of successful people who spoke about success. I would read books to create that intimate one-on-one environment in my bedroom. Over a period of 4 years on this journey of putting myself in this environment, I was bringing in $100K! It was not because I did anything special, but because of what my environment transformed me into over a period of time.

I used to be a rapper until I stopped hanging out with rappers. I used to curse often until I started hanging around people who don't curse. I used to love going to the club until I started hanging out with people who found the club very unproductive. I know what you're thinking: "David is just a follower—he just follows whatever the people he's around do." Well, in a sense I am okay with that, but the more you are in an environment, the more it impacts your beliefs. Why not make a conscious choice about what kind of environment you want to be in? My point is, whatever you want to become, find that environment and hang out for a while. Conversely, take a long look at what you DON'T want to become, and avoid putting yourself in that environment at all costs.

CHAPTER TEN

Dreams Are Built Overnight
-David Shands

So at this point, I've been simultaneously building my brand and working my job every single day of my life! I made a shirt called "No Days Off" that lists "No nights, no weekends, no half days, no birthdays, no snow days, no holidays…NO DAYS OFF!" I seriously lived this philosophy for 2½ years until the day I quit my job in October of 2012. I would work all day on my job and then work all night on my dream until it was time to go to work again the next morning. I would go to the club with a pocket full of wristbands that had Sleep is 4 Suckers on them and hand them out to anyone I made eye contact with. I was more into spreading the word than selling a product, and those silicon wristbands were the cheapest way to leave my message with someone who identified with the concept. I went so hard with wristband distribution that it wasn't long before 70% of my coworkers were wearing the bands daily. I gave packages of shirts to my cool DJ friends, I did a few fashion shows and blog interviews, and I bought a camera so I could shoot my own mini commercials. I would deliver shirts to my customers' houses after Thanksgiving dinner before they went to the club. I worked straight through my birthdays. It was sheer dedication. I showed my mother the "NO DAYS OFF" shirt, but she didn't agree with the design. She said "you need to relax at some point. You can't work all the time, David. Even God rested on the 7th day." I believe that wholeheartedly, but my response is unconventional. For one, the scriptures clearly state that one day to God is like 1,000 years to us. And even if His week were comprised of 7 24-hour days, would it not be aligned with His work ethic if you worked every day for 6 YEARS straight and took off the 7th year to travel the world, enjoy life, and create memories that would last a lifetime? Some people work 5 days each week and feel it necessary to take the other 2 days off. They feel that it's a better strategy to do this for 30 years at a job and eventually take off the next 20 years in retirement. I feel it's better for me to work 5 years straight and take off the next 2 years to have mini retirements along the way. Not being disrespectful, but I feel that the retirement lifestyle is much more enjoyable in your 20s, 30s, and 40s than in your 60s. Now, I'm not saying that retirement in your 60s isn't amazing because I'm not familiar with that experience, but I can only imagine.

    One day, I went to the Cheesecake Factory for lunch on my day off to enjoy my 25% off employee discount and sat at the bar, where my man Mike was bartending. Mike was a hustler for real. He was from New York, and he not only loved to make money, but he was also willing to work hard for it. Honestly, I never told him this, but his work ethic really inspired me to do more than what I was paid for. I saw him work his way from the bakery, putting cheesecakes on plates, to being a busboy, to being a barback helping out the bartenders, to being a bartender himself based simply on his work ethic. He did every job with intensity and style. As a result, he made more money than many of the servers, no matter what job he did.

    I'm not sure exactly how we got on the topic, but I began to tell Mike about this little clothing brand I started and how I worked on it during my days off. The next thing he said has stuck with me till this very day. We didn't talk about it long, but he said, "Yo son, you gotta have those $100 off-days like me." I put down my fork and asked him to elaborate. He said, "Yeah, my goal on every day I'm not behind this bar is to make at least $100. I plan on making money every day of my life, and if I'm not at work making money, it still has to get made. I'm gonna eat regardless!" We probably talked about this for no more than 30 seconds, but that was one of the most valuable conversations I've ever had. From that day on, I carried that with me and made it my own.

    I began to set the goal and track my progress. I began to gear up all week for those two days off from my job, including setting appointments to drop off shirts and running special promotions on my website. I ran up to barbershops and events with a box full of shirts in my back seat with this idea in my head that I can't go home until I make $100. What I found out is that it's very hard to hit a target that you can't see. Therefore, once I established the target, I began to work on hitting the bull's-eye. Before long, I was working 5 days on my job and 2 days on my dream, and I was making right around $100 during each day off. The entire $100 didn't come just off T-shirts, but the goal never changed. If I could make $20 by giving my friend a ride somewhere, another $40 off T-shirt sales, another $20 off wristbands, and a few bucks by being a "middleman" for printing someone else's shirts at the print shop I used, I did that. The method of making $100 was sometimes all over the place, but I never lost sight of the goal. It took a little time for me to consistently earn $100 on each day off, but it happened! When I actually realized what was happening, I asked my manager to only schedule me 4 days per week because I figured if I can make an extra $200 in 2 days, it's possible to make $300 in 3 days. It wasn't long before I was making $300 a week on my 3 days off. It was at this point that I got my first taste of the full-time entrepreneurship life. The idea of not having a job or a consistent guaranteed income to support me was very scary. Contrary to popular belief, I didn't just quit my job and put on my entrepreneur cape. I never jumped out of my comfort zone—I just slowly expanded it, and when I finally quit, it was just a calculated risk. I was only working 2 to 3 days per week at my job anyway by the time I quit because of this $100 Off-Day system I stole from Mike. I was making close to $500 a week outside of my job when I quit, so it wasn't a scary transition.

Let me put it this way: most people are so focused on wanting to be on the 2nd floor that they never study the staircase that links the 1st floor (where they are) to the 2nd floor (where they want to get to). We must get to a point where we stop looking at the 2nd floor, and we just focus on that 1st step. Most people think that the 1st step is insignificant, when in actuality the 1st step is the most critical in the whole process. After that 1st step, the 2nd step is the most critical step in the whole process, and so forth. People are so focused on replacing their salary that they never focus on just making a little extra per month CONSISTENTLY. Focus on making an extra $300 per month for 3 months with your part-time photography service. Focus on having your side business cover your car payment. Don't focus on quitting your job—just focus on that car payment. After that, you should be able to pay your car payment AND your light bill with the extra income from the little business you have going. If the goal is too big, it can be somewhat discouraging if you don't reach it. Even if you're making progress, you'll still get frustrated because you'll feel as though the progress is moving too slow. The tragedy of this scenario is that when frustration sets in, quitting altogether is right around the corner. Seeing is believing, and if you can just begin to see yourself knocking off daily or weekly goals, the progress is clearer to track, and feelings of gratification come more regularly.

I had a very clear advantage over most of my coworkers and friends. I was lucky enough to have people personally mentor me on all my business affairs. To and from work, I made sure I heard from my very wealthy friends. I was able to get advice from my mentor Jim Rohn, who would speak to me directly during my 30-minute commute to and from work. He loved me as his mentee so much that his consultation fee was only a one-time $9.99 audio download to my phone, and he would speak to me every day. I realized the power of being in the right environment and hearing the right information from the right people, so I bought as many audiobooks as I could find (because I hate reading). That was the closest I could get to a really successful person. I figured if these motivational speakers came to my house and sat in my living room, they would probably give me much of the same advice they had on their audio recording, so purchasing the tape and listening to it over and over again would serve the same purpose. Remember earlier in the book when I talked about how your environment will affect you before you affect it? How you will eventually pick up certain lingo, thought processes, ideas, etc., just by being in an environment long enough? Well, that's exactly what began to happen as I listened to all these positive words every day…ALL DAY! I found myself using certain words that my "mentors" used—giving my friends advice using word-for-word lines from these audiobooks and YouTube video clips I watched every day after work. I even picked up a small accent and developed a different speech pattern by creating that environment around me.

At this point, I was growing personally at a tremendous rate, and my business was starting to take shape, but I still didn't have a live mentor I could call and hang out with. The audio recordings and YouTube videos were great, but I still felt as though I needed someone I could pick up the phone and call with specific questions—someone who would mentor me personally. The reason these speakers and life coaches make audio recordings is because they don't have the time, nor the desire, to mentor people like me by giving away information they had to struggle to obtain. These people charge thousands of dollars to consult with companies, and I couldn't possibly pay that kind of money for a conversation. My audio/visual mentor Jim Rohn gave me the answer one day, and it started something for me that allowed me to wiggle my way into very valuable relationships. Jim suggested "taking a rich guy to lunch." At first when I heard it, I thought that was odd. Why would I pay for food for a millionaire when picking up a $40 tab would have a more significant impact on my pockets than it would on theirs? If I ever sat down with someone whom I knew made an admirable income in my eyes, when the bill came, I would be inclined to just wait for them to reach for it first, silently hoping they'd say something like 'Don't worry about it—lunch is on me." However what I realized is that successful people are successful because of the things they do. And people who are unsuccessful are unsuccessful for the same reasons. I began to see that if the things I did could get me the things I wanted, I would already have them, so I decided to change my philosophy about free lunch. I simply began to invite!

I stated earlier that I began to change my environment and began to engage with people who were more successful than me. This was one of my actics for making that happen. Anyone I ran into who made the kind of money I wanted to make, I would offer to take them to lunch and make sure to stress that the meal was on me. Through this process, I learned three things: 1) rich people rarely turn down a free lunch; 2) rich people love to talk about their expertise on a subject and appreciate someone noticing how smart they are; and 3) rich people don't mind helping people with ambition, especially if you remind them of themselves before they experienced success. At the Cheesecake Factory, I began to study my guests. I would serve some pretty sharp people whom I could just tell had money by the way they spoke, dressed, and interacted with me. My "wealth radar" was on point most of the time, and if I suspected that they were someone I would like as a mentor, I would pop the question!

Here was my approach: after I interviewed them by asking questions about their profession to see if they would qualify to be my mentor (cocky, I know), I would say, "Wow, you're one of the most brilliant and successful people I've ever met in my life. I aspire to be more than just a server at this restaurant. I have no problem refilling your drinks and making sure you enjoy your dining experience, but I feel that God has called me to do something much greater than this. I know you're extremely busy, but I was wondering if I could take you to lunch sometime? I admire you as a businessman, and I have very few people in my life whom I admire. The information I could learn from you during lunch would be far more valuable than the money I would spend on the meal, but it's all I've got." Insert slow violin music playing in the background. I promise you, it worked like a charm!

People like to be admired and love to be recognized for the success they have achieved. Top that with a free meal, and most of the time the answer will be yes. The secret is to get them to like you. And listening to the audio version of *How to Win Friends and Influence People* by Dale Carnegie allowed me to pick up certain people skills that taught me how to win friends. During most of the conversations I have with people, I reserve my opinions and simply ask questions. I discovered that people love to talk about themselves and give advice. I'm not saying it's out of arrogance, but people are opinionated by nature. I discovered that if I had a conversation with someone and they talked the entire time, they would walk away saying, "Man, we had a great conversation." Now, you and I know that it wasn't really a conversation—they just talked the whole time—but they would walk away remembering that great conversation that you all had. Become INTERESTED before trying to be so INTERESTING. People don't care about how much you know until they know how much you care. Asking questions shows that you genuinely care about who they are and that you value their conversation. Respond to each question with an answer that is immediately followed by a question. Get the conversation off of YOU and back to the other person as soon as possible. There are so many things you can do to get successful people to like you, but this bit will get you the date.

After these people made the commitment to do lunch with me (based on my "young, Black, inner-city kid trying to make it" story), half the battle was over. I would find out what side of town they would like to meet and what kind of food they liked. And 99% of the time they didn't even care about the food, but I always made sure the location was geographically convenient for them so they wouldn't be going out of their way. After I figured out which side of town, I'd have to find the spot. Because I was on a VERY tight budget, I would do extensive research on food spots in the area. I didn't want to pick fast food, but we weren't going to Ruth's Chris Steak House either. I wanted to find a very inexpensive restaurant that was budget-friendly but not McDonald's, which would make me seem cheap. I found that there are some very comfortable sandwich spots, gourmet burger joints, or other places that have an inexpensive lunch menu. My goal was to spend no more than $25, so in Atlanta, I would take them to places like Chipotle, Fellini's Pizza, or little boutique restaurants. You may or may not believe me but this one strategy alone has opened so many doors for me that I am still in shock. I would take notes right at the table, showing true interest and demonstrating that the information these people were giving me was valuable. Being truly interested in them made all the difference in the world. They began to invite me to private events, introduce me as their mentee, and link me up with people who could help me. And, of course, the conversations just between the two of us were extremely valuable on their own.

This principle alone, if applied, could be the difference maker for you. This has been my strategy for building a laundry list of mentors I can call at will. I still have very powerful lunches with millionaires and successful business owners on a regular basis, and if you knew all my mentors, you would be able to see a bit of each of them in my style, my conversations, the advice I give, and the way I handle business. Here's the best part: I have people ask to pick my brain all the time, and I tell them to take me to lunch and I got you. The funny thing is, people who don't know me personally have no problem with that, but some people who knew me when I was a server get upset and say I'm "acting Hollywood now" or say things like, "You're going to make me pay for your food just to get advice from you, David? Are you serious? You make enough money to pay for your own meal." I actually understand the response as well as their reservation because I used to think that way, but I'm at a point now where I value my time and I finally understand why these speakers charge thousands of dollars to consult with businesses and do life coaching. I love to give and pour into others, especially my close friends, but if they don't value their business enough to invest in information, it's a waste of my time and theirs because success will continue to elude them for having the wrong mindset. Now that I no longer take food for payment, I've placed a monetary value on the time I spend with those who claim they want to be successful and help guide them in the development of their businesses.

CHAPTER TWELVE

Outgrow YOUR Business

Dreams Are Built Overnight
-David Shands

Contrary to popular belief, my main focus is not on growing and developing my business; my main focus is on growing and developing as a person. I tell people all the time that I spend more time expanding my mind through education than I do expanding my business; consequently, the business grows by default. What I've learned is that your business cannot grow past your own level of thinking. In the event that your business outgrows you, generally it will eventually fold back into your own level of understanding and problem solving; it's only a matter of time. Becoming a billionaire is not a financial goal for me—it's a developmental goal. My goal is not to earn a billion dollars to become a billionaire; my goal is to become a person who thinks and achieves on a level that 99.9967% of the world doesn't. Do you know what kind of person you have to be to earn a billion dollars? Do you understand the level of problems that must be solved to earn a billion dollars? A billionaire becomes a billionaire because of the person that they have become, the knowledge they have gained, the sizable problems they are able to solve, and the necessary disciplines they have adopted that have manifested materially into monetary value.

As soon as I began to develop this thought process, I immediately wanted to start working on self-development. I started reading books and challenging myself to achieve more. I even used my job as a server to work on myself. Working as a server, my job was to interact with the public, so what better training ground could I have had to improve my people skills? I started to realize how often my colleagues and I would blame everyone but ourselves for why we received bad tips.

Some of us would blame the bartenders for not making the drinks fast enough or blame the kitchen cooks for preparing the food incorrectly. We would quite often blame management for not providing all the resources we needed in order to receive good tips. If the food came out perfectly, the bartenders made the drinks without fault, and management provided everything we needed, and if the tables consistently left bad tips that evening, some of us would even be inclined to walk straight up to the host desk and blame them for seating us with the wrong type of guests, as if they had some kind of psychic ability to know how much tip guests would leave. When all else failed, we would just call the guests cheap or ghetto (behind their backs, of course) or any other label we could use for what was wrong with them for not leaving us a good tip.

    I had a serious mindset shift as I embarked on this personal development journey. Instead of thinking of my current job as a problem, I looked at it as an opportunity to be "faithful over few." I had to do my best and be the best at what I was doing in order for God to propel me to the next level. I started to study top leaders and successful people, and what I began to realize is that my income was directly linked to the size of the problems I could solve. When I realized that, I became obsessed with problem solving. I stopped looking at my guests as tips and began to look at them as opportunities to develop my people skills. I began to pay attention to body language. I began to guide people through their dining experience rather than letting them just pick a dish off the menu that I would go fetch for them. I began to study the guests. I began to feel when people wanted me to be very interactive, and I also knew when they wanted their space. I began to be a chameleon with each guest and to understand that people are attracted to people who are like themselves. If they talked fast, I spoke fast. If they talked slowly, I would slow down my speech pattern. If they were very professional, so was I. If they were real laid back and chill, I would mimic that to a degree. It got to the point where this job had nothing to do with making money; instead, I felt as though I was in a people skills training course that I was getting paid to attend. I figured if I couldn't solve a problem as small as making sure someone enjoyed their dining experience in a place that they voluntarily walked into, I would never be able to solve billionaire problems. Sometimes it would take a manager walking over to a table to put out a fire and make sure a disgruntled guest was going to leave as a satisfied customer. Those guys made $40,000 to $60,000 annually, and if I couldn't solve the problems that they can easily solve, I would never get past $20,000.

Check this out: it got so intense that I even used that job to work on my speech. Every server had a welcoming spiel that went something like this: "Hello, my name is David. The soup of the day is clam chowder. Also, the fish of the day are salmon and mahi-mahi, which comes with broccoli and mashed potatoes. I can start with your drink order, if you'd like." As you're reading my welcoming pitch, you are probably thinking to yourself that it's a pretty standard pitch for a restaurant, and since I said the same thing 30 times per day for years (they never changed the fish of the day in all my 6 years), I could probably recite this pitch in my sleep. However, the problem is that I have always had a slight issue with slurring my words. Since I could recite this phrase backward, I never even had to think about it, so it would come out very lazy. It sounded more like, "Hello, my name is David. The fish uh the day is salmon 'n' mahi-mahi, which comes wit broccoli 'n' mashed potatoes. I can start wit ya drink order, if you'd like." Once I realized how much I did that, I began to enunciate my words intentionally. I knew I would be a speaker one day, so it only made sense to start practicing at my job. I turned my "fish uh the day" into "fish OF the day" and my "wit" into "with." It was such a slight adjustment that I'm sure no one but me noticed; but the discipline and adjustments I made that year took me from making $20,000/year to $30,000/year just like that! I decided to work on myself instead of working on getting better tips. My income magically multiplied, and it has continued to do so every year since.

  I encourage you to get more from your job than just a paycheck. If all you get from your job is money, you will be there forever—or until they fire you, or until you find another job that may possibly pay you more money. Most people use the excuse that their job is too demanding, and they don't have time to work on their dream because they work so many hours at their job. I began to realize that working on my dream is useless if I am not working on myself. With that said, I was determined to find a way to work on my future by working on myself while I was at work, as opposed to working solely on my job while I was at work.

  I started to really use my job to my advantage. I started off selling the Sleep is 4 Suckers wristbands, and guess who were my first customers? My coworkers! I would come to work showing them the latest designs, and their opinions ultimately decided whether or not each design went to print. My first few photo shoots included coworkers. When I threw my first events, guess who I reached out to? My coworkers rocked with the brand so heavy, almost all the servers were wearing the wristbands! It got so bad that a district manager came in and noticed it on everyone's wrist and banned the wearing of it. I guess the whole "Suckers" thing wasn't too professional, but I didn't get upset at all. I was excited that we made enough noise to gain the attention of upper management.

    Most people think I'm exaggerating when I say I LOVED working at the Cheesecake Factory, but now you can see why. I got all my good ideas, free modeling services, free market research from the opinions of my coworkers, and, to top it all off, I got personality and problem-solving training, speech training, great support, capital investment (from my tips), and of course a free meal every now and then! How could you hate your job when it provides all that? The problem is, some people are so caught up in the fact that they hate their job that they miss the opportunities to grow and get paid for it.

CHAPTER THIRTEEN

Dreams Are Built Overnight
-David Shands

Building a brand is an art. Building a brand is not about selling a product—it's more about painting a picture. If you were to sell a good product, customers would appreciate it, but they would end up consuming it and only remembering what the product did for them. If your customers find a similar product with better results, you will never see them again. If your customers can find a similar product for a cheaper price, even if your product is superior, you'd be surprised at how many people would rather save money on "close enough." That is why for YEARS I bought generic cereal instead of the name brand stuff. Tootie Fruities don't taste exactly like Fruit Loops, but hey, they are not half bad. Seriously, Fruity Dyno-Bites look and feel just like Fruity Pebbles; they taste somewhat similar, and other than the fact that they get soggy as soon as they touch the milk, they are a pretty good bargain. Those large companies have not given me enough reasons to care about supporting their brand. On the other hand, Girl Scouts, in my opinion, do not make the best cookies I have ever had in my life, but every year I buy a minimum of 10 boxes. The cookies are good, but it's the story of the Girl Scouts that I find so fascinating. The idea of little girls being mentored by women, and kids getting their first crack at entrepreneurship is a beautiful thing to me. Even the boxes tell the story. The images on the boxes are always of women teaching young girls a valuable lesson or doing something productive and fun. Girl Scouts have been masters at painting a picture for their customers, so much so that people stock up on these cookies, which are offered only once a year. I don't like ANYTHING with coconut in it AT ALL, but if a little girl approaches me with a couple of boxes of that chocolate-covered coconut cookie thing, and that is ALL the Girl Scout has at the time, I am inclined to buy the darn things anyway. Reason being, I am not buying the cookies—I am buying the idea, or in other words, their painting.

    When I first began building the Sleep is 4 Suckers brand, we worked hard on the logo and the first design. We made a bunch of changes, and we finally came up with the final look. We put the Sleep is 4 Suckers logo on the back of the neck, really small and fashionable, and we made the design on the front slightly bigger, enough that you can see the details. I was so excited because I have never seen a design so beautiful, and it was all mine! I could not wait to get these shirts printed because I knew they would sell out immediately. I printed 72 T-shirts, knowing that wasn't going to be enough, but that was all the money I had. I was so concerned that they would sell out too fast, so I had a sit-down with the print shop owner to make a deal. I said, "Listen, bro, how fast can I get more shirts printed after these sell out? It's only going to take a few days to sell them once they're released, and I need priority printing to keep this thing rolling. I'll probably be your #1 client, dumping A LOT of money into your business, so if you can take care of me, I'll make you my exclusive printer! I need your personal cell number so I can have direct access to you." You should have seen my face! My posture and the way I crossed my legs; I was sitting back in the chair as if I were Ralph Lauren himself! The air of arrogance was so thick in the room that you could feel it, but the beauty of the design was assurance that it would be a big hit. Before I even got the shirts printed, I showed all my friends and family, and they felt the same way. I had

GUARANTEED orders from everyone I showed them to. All my coworkers said, "Let me know when you get those in. I NEED that!" Not to mention the fact that I got them printed on the highest quality American Apparel blank shirts that I could find. I was so happy when I finally got the shirts in; they looked exactly how I imagined they would. It was game time!

After about 2 weeks I had only sold about 8 shirts, and I could not figure out why! The design and shirt quality were amazing! All the friends, family, and coworkers who had made a commitment to buy either brushed me off or asked for free shirts so they could "promote" my brand for me. I used to HATE the word "promote." They would say things like, "Dave, I'm telling you, if you gave me one, I'd wear it and EVERYONE would want to know where I got it from." If I heard it once, I heard it a million times. No one found my product valuable enough to pay for it; they all wanted it for free. I was so frustrated! I think my pastor bought two for himself and his wife, the girl I was dating at the time bought one, along with my best friend, Brandon, and a few other people; but most of my sales were just for support. I felt like a charity case.

I had to face the apparent fact that my first shirt design wasn't as groundbreaking as I thought it was. The only thing people kept saying when they turned the shirt around to see the logo was, "Sleep is 4 Suckers? That's my life. I live that phrase." After hearing that enough, I had to re-evaluate my whole approach. I began leading with the name of the brand instead of the design. I stopped trying to point out the details of the design and telling them how this color was in season, having them feel the quality of the shirt, and asking them to try it on so they could feel how it fit them perfectly. Instead, I began to just sell the Sleep is 4 Suckers concept. I explained to them my belief that sleep was more of a mental condition than an act, and that if you give up a bit of sleep, you can have everything you desire. If you are willing to give up a bit of leisure, pass on happy hour, and consistently grind with all that you have in you for a short period of time, your dreams can become a reality. Before I even brought the shirt out of the "back seat boutique" (as I affectionately called my office aka my car), I would tell them what Sleep is 4 Suckers meant and why I was willing to give up sleep to accomplish my goals. Before I even showed them the design, they were already sold on the concept because most people could identify with what I was saying. The shirts began to sell at a faster pace. My closing ratio quadrupled, and I began to have a real business going. I discounted that first run of shirts and gave a bunch away because I had a new brilliant idea for the next shirt!

After a couple of months, I saved enough money to start my second run. I found some comparable blank shirts that were much less expensive than the high-quality American Apparel shirts that I had used previously, but they were still of good material. For the next design, I took the small "Si4S" logo from the back of the shirt and placed it as big as I could on the front of the shirt. I then simply spelled out Sleep is 4 Suckers across the back. People really got excited about that! My customers told me that it was somewhat of a conversation piece and that they were spreading the word through deep conversation about what that phrase meant to them, similar to how I sold the shirt to that initial customer. It was great because my customers were going out and promoting to other potential customers, not because of a shirt design but because of an idea, a philosophy, a concept...a "picture" that I began painting. I am so grateful that my first design sucked because it forced me to start painting. It forced me to give people more than one reason to buy a shirt, similar to the Girl Scout cookies. Some people will buy the shirt because they like the person selling it. Some will buy the shirt because they like the name. Others will buy the shirt because it is Black owned or because they see themselves reflected in the concept. Some people will buy the shirt because they know someone else who lives the Sleep is 4 Suckers lifestyle, and a few people will buy the shirt because they need something to match their new sneakers! People may also buy the shirt because the shirt is a reminder of a 15-minute conversation we had about why God put them on this earth, and how you cannot "sleep" on your own potential, and how your sleeping (laziness) will never provide your family the lifestyle they deserve. Once they took this shirt home with them, that conversation would last forever. I realized that the more reasons people have to do something, the more inclined they are to do it. So in my presentation, I go over all the reasons you should buy into this movement, and out of those 10 reasons, I am sure to catch you with 1. As of now, we are at a level where people really like the designs and shirt quality, but that is just a bonus.

In my retail locations, my team and I will have deep conversations, bringing people literally to tears by telling them about the company and what we represent, before we say one thing about a shirt. After the conversation, our potential customers say things like, "I gotta get a shirt. Let me find one," which is odd, if you think about it. Generally, when you go shopping, you will find a shirt that you like, check the price tag, and make sure the color goes with the shoes or outfit that you want to wear it with. After you find what you are looking for, you take it to the register and pay. However, at our store, people make a decision to buy our product even before they find one that they like! Our brand is just different.

When you begin painting pictures and sell a story along with the product, the story will remain long after customers have used the product or service. They may forget how good your cupcakes tasted, or forget how well you cut their hair, or forget how you made them look when you did their makeup, but they will never forget how your story made them feel. If your story can affect someone emotionally, you've got a client for life. Package your story and make it powerful. Do not ever let a customer or client leave without your story. If they truly buy your story, you will never have to worry about them buying your product; they will spend the money by default. I haven't sold T-shirts since that first design run. I sell people an idea…they just end up giving me a donation for the shirts.

CHAPTER FOURTEEN

Dreams Are Built Overnight
-David Shands

Going from your job to your dream is no easy task. Looking back over my life, this journey has been the most challenging, educational, exhausting, and fulfilling time of my life, and I remember the process vividly. I could wrap up all that's necessary to succeed in a single word...SACRIFICE!

This word, in its true definition, is a hard pill to swallow—so much so that people often redefine the word to make it more comfortable to do. The word "sacrifice" by definition generally involves the death of something or the total release of something very valuable to you. You can't cut back on luxuries that you can do without and call it a sacrifice. If you're familiar with the story of Abraham, you know that God asked him to sacrifice his son Isaac. Here is how we know it was a true sacrifice for Abraham: God felt it necessary to say, "Take your son...your ONLY son...whom you LOVE, and SACRIFICE him." God didn't ask him to offer up 1 of his 5 kids, and He didn't tell Abraham to find a random boy to slaughter. I believe there's a reason He didn't fail to mention very descriptively that this was someone very, very special and precious to Abraham. I'm not saying you have to offer up your firstborn to be successful, but you WILL have to give up something valuable, trust me. The law of sacrifice applies across the board in all industries. Ask any kingpin drug dealer who considers himself successful if he's ever sacrificed anything to get where he is, whether it be his life or freedom, and record his answer. Ask the founder and CEO of any company or any star athlete in any major sports league about their sacrifices and record the answer. The stories get very interesting, to say the least. Record all these answers and you'll probably find a common thread that's shared by the CEO, the drug dealer, and the athlete on the topic of sacrifice. I'm not saying that what I'm telling you is a fact, or that it's even true—it's simply an educated opinion based on my own research. So what I'm telling you is to not take my opinion as the truth but instead to do your own independent study of successful people. If, and only if, you find what I found about the law of true sacrifice, the rest of this chapter will make much more sense.

Now that we're on the same page about sacrifice and we agree that sacrifice is an ingredient that many successful people have seasoned their journey with, a very serious question should arise: what will be your sacrifice? A sacrifice is something of value that is killed and offered up to a deity to pledge their faith. A sacrifice demonstrates that I believe wholeheartedly in this deity and I'm pledging my allegiance to it through faith by releasing something I value for the sake of the deity. The offering has nothing to do with the deity itself, and it's not as though the deity needs your offering for its personal use, but the ceremony has more to do with the one doing the sacrifice. Now, before this chapter gets too weird, replace the word "deity" with whatever the name of your goal is right now. Anything worth having will require a sacrifice, and when I understood this, I began to create a sacrifice list. One of the things on my list was the celebration of my birthday. While I worked at the restaurant, I vowed not to celebrate my birthday in any way until my business allowed me to quit my job. For two years straight, I was even reluctant to tell anyone that it was my birthday because I felt that I didn't deserve to celebrate it. In fact, I decided to begin buying my mother a gift every year for MY birthday. That was my sacrifice for attaining my goal. Fortunately, the tradition of getting my mother a gift every year for my birthday has never stopped. Another sacrifice was television; I refused to even own cable during this period of going from my job to my dream. The tradition of not paying a cable bill ended about 2 years after I quit, but the habit is still there. Even though I have cable now, I rarely even turn on my TV. One of my mentors told me about how he loved to play basketball, but he told himself that he wouldn't shoot a ball until he replaced his six-figure job income with a six-figure income from home. Needless to say, he's an avid ball player now. So again I ask, what's your sacrificial offering to your dream? I'm asking you to dig deep now. Find something that would be very uncomfortable for you to give up, and do it!

Most people never become successful simply because they don't have enough reasons to. I'm asking you to not go on vacation until you've reach a certain benchmark, and no matter how bad you want to take that girls' trip, your dedication to that sacrificial offering says that you can't. You'll eventually get so sick of missing out on trips, or not celebrating your birthday, or not being able to drink your favorite wine, that it just adds one more item to the list of reasons to work harder. Without some good reasons to succeed, you'll find a lot more reasons that being average is not that bad. You simply need reasons. So before you flip another page, I would like you to write down your sacrificial offerings and stick to them. Here's what I'm aware of: 95% of people reading this book will actually write down what they're willing to give up, but as soon as that urge hits them, they take that sacrifice back from their deity and use it for themselves. It's like tithing to your church and 3 days later asking for it back. Stick to your decision and become a part of the 5% who produce real fruit from this exercise.

Some people have the unique ability to dream dreams and have visions. God has given you a glimpse—a very small glimpse—of who you will become, and you are excited about walking into that position and purpose. God said it, you believe it, and now you are just waiting to receive it. You are waiting for it to come to pass as God said it would because of your faith, which is commendable. Some even ask God to send them a sign to be sure that what they saw was truly from God. Some receive the vision and pray about it and ask God for the next step. Philippians 4:6 in the New Living Translation reads: "Don't worry about anything; instead, pray about everything. Tell God what you need, and thank Him for all He has done." The bible also says that He will supply all my needs, while at the same time, the bible says that a man who does not work does not eat. I recently spoke to someone about his goals and what his next step is going to be. He told me that he is very talented in various areas, but he has been trying to figure out which avenue is going to create the wealth that God said he would have. He said he has been praying about it and is just waiting for God to guide him in the direction he should go.

Now, I do not want this chapter to make you think that I rely on my own ability to create success. In fact, this whole journey with God has been a supernatural experience. The moves I make that I don't have the ability or intelligence to make, and that happen to work out miraculously in my favor—that's all Him. The fact that I am a public speaker who captivates an audience with no formal training, using words that I cannot spell nor clearly define, is a miracle in itself. I am in awe of how far God has taken me and how blessed I am in spite of how much I don't deserve it. I have disappointed and lied to God so often, it's ridiculous. I am totally dependent on God to guide my path, however in my experience, He has guided the path that I decided to take. My prayer was for Him to guide my path and to let it be pleasing in His sight. Honestly, I do not think God really cares whether I sell T-shirts or real estate. I do not think God really cares whether you take this job or that job, major in science or telecommunications, or go to this school or that; I just do not think He cares. I asked God to direct the path of whatever path I choose, as long as it is being used to glorify Him.

Is it possible that I could quit public speaking, selling clothes, and teaching entrepreneurship workshops, and just get a job as a schoolteacher and still be in God's will as long as I am working? Or would that be considered disobedient? I get frustrated when my friend tells me that he is waiting for God to tell him which of his gifts he is supposed to use. If you were a gifted musician and also a gifted writer, would you be out of the will of God for life to just pick one and do it and have God direct your path in that gift that you choose to operate in? I really feel that it is either laziness or fearfulness that prevents people from moving forward. They would rather wait for God to smack them in the mouth with a note saying, "Do this," knowing that there is only a small possibility that they will literally wake up with a sticky note attached to their lips signed by God Himself. They would rather place the blame on the person they pray to, as if they are waiting on Him and that the reason they have not moved is because God didn't do His part yet. God did not whisper in my ear and say, "David, I want you to start this clothing brand, and I want you to call it Sleep 4 Suckers." All He gave me was a glimpse of who I am. God gave me a vision of what I can do and who I can become, but He did not give me a turn-by-turn road map as to how to get there. The scripture says "Whatever your hands findeth to do, do it with all thy might…" It did NOT say, "Whatever 'I' tell you to do or whatever you think 'I' am telling you to do"—it says, "Whatever YOUR hands findeth to do.' Whatever YOUR hands touch, whatever business YOU decide to pick up, whatever hobby YOU get involved in, whoever YOU decide to engage in a marriage with, whatever path YOU choose, do THAT work with all your might. Just pick something and give it your all. Chances are you won't be doing that work forever anyway.

I remember when I was in a network marketing company called Pre-Paid Legal Services, and I went HARD! I went to every meeting; I read every book that my up-line suggested. They introduced me to a concept called "personal development." Although I did not consult with God about whether or not I should sign up with the company, it ultimately brought me closer to Him. I tried to recruit my pastor into the company, and although he declined my invitation, he liked that I would get more into reading and becoming a better person. I read a book that was going to help me understand the psychology of people, called *How to Win Friends and Influence People*. I figured if I could understand people, I would be able to recruit them more efficiently, ultimately getting me closer to becoming the wealthy man God showed me I could become. I visited my pastor one day, and I happened to have that book in my hand. He looked at the book for a second and said, "You think all these books you are reading have something to do with Pre-Paid Legal and recruiting people, huh?"

At the time, I am thinking to myself, "Of course—why else would I read these books? I wanna get rich, recruit more people, and become a top money earner in the company like my mentor. He said these are the books that helped him do it and that they would help me, too." I only made about $15,000 in that company, but years later I am still reading those books and recommending them to people. Even today, I still apply the principles I learned when I was recruiting people: keep the people excited, teach the people the business, and build the people into great leaders. My mentor Mr. Jonathan Green would call it "layered leadership;" not only teaching people how to be leaders, but also teaching them how to teach others to lead. I use this in my own companies to this very day. Pastor Borom was right—those books had nothing to do with the company I was in, but they had everything to do with who I would become. I had no idea that I could go from working at the Cheesecake Factory, to building a clothing line while working there, to quitting the job and going full-time with clothing, to being booked with speaking engagements, to writing a book about how I went from working at the Cheesecake Factory to building a clothing line! God did not tell me all of that before I started. All I know is that God did not create me to be average, and when He put me together and planted me on this earth, He had some expectations in mind. I could be wrong, but I do not think God cares whether I am a middle school gym teacher or a world-renowned motivational speaker as long as "whatever I findeth my hands to do," I do it with all my might and I somehow usher people who live in darkness into the marvelous light. I give Him all the glory throughout this process. He's a happy God!

CHAPTER SIXTEEN

BLIND FAITH

Dreams Are Built Overnight
-David Shands

I had a few people tell me that they didn't like the name, they didn't like the quality, they didn't like the designs, and they didn't like the logo, but I kept pushing. A few people told me that no one would agree with me that Sleep is 4 Suckers, because scientifically we all need sleep, but I pushed the message anyhow. They told me that kids wouldn't be able to wear the shirts in school because of the "Suckers" part…But GOD! One of the keys to my success is my consistency and my faith in what I heard, not what I'm hearing. I kept faith in what I saw, not what I'm currently seeing. Allow me to explain.

One of my favorite shirts from the Sleep is 4 Suckers brand is the "Blind Faith" design. It is a picture of a woman wearing a blindfold, and the blindfold has the word "FAITH" written across it. This shirt means a lot to me because my entire life has been a faith walk, seeing as how I'm not exactly qualified by the world's standards to do a lot of the things that God has allowed me to do. I noticed a genuine need for mentorship in high schools, so I began to go to the schools. I came to the realization that some people never become successful because they have no real-life examples of success. When I was in school, someone's older brother who had his own apartment, drove a used car, and made $18/hour had true wealth to me because that's the best I had ever seen. These kids have no examples of success at home, at school, or at church of anyone who had a dream and achieved it, so I went. I began to bring my entrepreneur friends to the schools to give these kids a real-life picture of young business owners who have become or who are in the process of becoming who they want to be. We named it "The Black Wall Street Tour" after the historical Black Wall

Street that originated in Tulsa, Oklahoma in the early 1900s, which was a segregated neighborhood comprised of young African American professionals, leaders, and entrepreneurs. One gentleman asked me how long I've been a certified counselor. I looked at the guy as though he had 2 heads and asked, "What do you mean?"

He said, "They just let you walk into high schools without a certification and let you teach, counsel, and train their students whenever you want?"

I said, "Yup." I simply knew by faith what I heard God say, and I walked in it. The challenge is when your eyes don't agree with what God shows you—meaning your vision was clear when you saw what He showed you, but all your sight sees now are obstacles. You caught a glimpse of your future lifestyle, but all you can see now is your current living situation. You saw a vision of your promise at one point, but all you can see now are your problems. The old phrase "Out of sight, out of mind" had it right, which also means those things that are "in sight" are "in mind." If you allow what you see today to cloud your vision of what you saw when God originally gave you the vision, you'll never have it. "Seeing is believing," as the old phrase goes, and it couldn't be a more real truth. I saw God give me my own business. While I was still serving tables, He showed me a glimpse of going from an employee to an employer. The problem is that people get so caught up in what they see—bills, circumstances, kids, an unsupportive spouse, and so on—that they forget what they saw (the vision). You heard in your heart 5 years ago that you should write a book; a voice spoke to you and you heard what your purpose is, but all you can hear now is the creditors calling, your boss telling you to work overtime, or your teachers telling you that if you don't attend college you won't amount to anything, and it drowns out what you heard in your spirit. It takes STRONG faith—BLIND faith—to believe that you can achieve more in spite of seemingly insurmountable odds.

For those who don't understand the whole "faith" thing, I'm going to attempt to help you gain some understanding. An abbreviated definition of faith is the evidence of things not seen. Faith is evidence that what you can't see is really there, which is a developed perspective. Faith is having a KNOWING that where you see yourself is where you will be; it only depends on which lens you're looking through. Conspiracy theorists, for example, can find evidence in EVERYTHING that the government is conspiring to kill us all off. The evidence is so clear to them in everything they see that they have an answer for every rebuttal. When they prove their point, it's so clear to them that they are having a hard time understanding how you can't see what they're saying. Pessimists always find EVIDENCE that things will turn out in a negative way. They can point out every negative component in every situation, and the evidence is crystal clear. So when it comes to faith, you have to look at your dreams through a more optimistic lens and point out how everything in your life is working together for your good. Just like the conspiracy theorist, what kind of evidence in your life can you focus on that proves you will be who you want to be? I found out that every great leader was a public servant. Every leader in history became great at serving others, and I found it no coincidence that God allowed me to be a server at a restaurant. Now that may be reaching, and it may be silly or weird to some people. Some may discount it as a coincidence, but in my heart, I found EVIDENCE in every area of my life that I would be the leader of many.

I think most people who are reading this book would like to have faith in the outcome, faith in the process, and most importantly, faith in themselves, but it's hard to have faith when your reality appears to be so real. How can you expect to write a book when you failed almost every English and literature class you've ever taken? How will you ever make six figures when the only skill you've acquired is serving tables? If I can't seem to pay my own bills, how can I expect to pay my mother's? These are questions that I asked myself every day before I changed my lens and started looking for evidence. The pain and emotional torture feel and look so real that it's hard to have faith in an outcome that is so far beyond where you are, but I think I can help a bit.

Faith comes from belief. As I said earlier, the cliché "Seeing is believing" is a very true statement; so if belief in your own success comes from seeing it, you have to create small wins for yourself to SEE more often. I used to think I could never win because I was so used to losing. I never got any awards growing up. I never won a spelling bee, I never won a championship trophy, and I never won any of the games or prizes at amusement parks. Out of all the jobs I've ever had, I never received an employee of the month award. I have had a really bad losing streak, but when I realized that the only way to have faith is to believe, and to believe I must see, I started creating small "wins" that I could SEE every day. I would create a task list, and if I completed the task list for the day, I considered that "winning" the day. If I left some things incomplete, I lost. So I started out with easily attainable goals, such as:

1. Contact a web designer
2. Make a list of 5 T-shirt concepts
3. Go grocery shopping
4. Clean my room
5. Call Mom
6. Research different marketing methods

I got accustomed to "winning" on a regular basis. I was knocking these out of the park, and that's when I adopted the philosophy of "Execution Over Excuses." If it was 11:55 p.m. and I hadn't yet struck a line through the "Call Mom" task, she was going to get a call with total disregard for her sleep schedule. I got so used to "beating" the day that I started stretching myself and putting more difficult tasks on my list, like "Sell 3 T-shirts today" or "Make $150 in tips at work" or "Meet someone of influence today." Accomplishing these tasks led me to believe that I could accomplish greater ones. Sounds crazy, right?

Back in school, I would rarely complete my homework; I would complete just enough class assignments to barely pass almost every year of my school career. This reality caused me to repeat phrases like "I can't do homework" and "I don't do well in school." Because I DIDN'T do well in school, it led me to believe that I COULDN'T do well in school. What I saw became my belief. I became an executor simply by executing. You may have to start small, but these small wins build your faith in yourself as an executor. My father use to say things like "If you can make a dime, you can make a dollar," meaning if you have the ability to make a dollar once, you can do it twice and eventually have $2 in your possession. If you make that dollar often enough, you'll end up with $10 in no time. In the beginning, you may not have faith in your ability to make $10, but the simple task of accumulating that single buck is right on your level. If you do that often enough, your faith in your ability to do more builds, but you have to start at your belief level. I don't teach kids that they can make a million dollars or that they can become a millionaire for 2 reasons: one, because I myself am not a millionaire yet (though by the time you actually read this book, depending on when you read it, this fact may have changed), and two, they wouldn't believe me if I told them. If I were to ask kids, "Who in this class is going to be a millionaire when they grow up?" every student in attendance would raise their hand, but sadly they wouldn't really believe it. You mean to tell me that a child in an inner city school who has lived in lack their whole life, never even met a millionaire in real life, hears "struggle" talk from every adult they have ever come in contact with, and has no examples at home or school of anyone even making a decent income, really believes they are going to accomplish the seemingly un-accomplishable? Man, PLEASE! That's too far of a stretch for them. As a matter of fact, I've found that the older you get, the less you believe in your own ability to succeed, so it's an even further stretch for adults to believe.

So here is my goal: to get people to have faith that they can accomplish just a little more than they have accomplished thus far. I have to get kids to believe that they can go from failing to passing. Not all A's, but just passing. If they can remember a time when they were failing, and now they're passing, they now have a story to encourage not only others that improvement is possible, but they can also encourage themselves. If I can show them that they can do just a little more than what they've done, they'll always believe they can do even more. This same principle applies to you. Keep the faith in that dream God showed you rather than the nightmare you are currently seeing, and walk in the vision that is set forth. See past what your eyes are telling you, and keep the vision in front of you.

CHAPTER SEVENTEEN

Dreams Are Built Overnight
-David Shands

I'm positive that this book has provided a certain level of motivation and education to everyone who has read it. People all across the world will leave their jobs and live fulfilled lives because of one or many of the principles in this book. These practical applications are easy for anyone to follow. I know this because I teach both middle school and high school kids as well as people who have been in the work-force for over 30 years the same exact principles that are outlined throughout these chapters. They work for both demographics and every demographic in between.

I want to inform you, however, that the information provided isn't the most valuable component of this book. Anyone who has known me since high school or college will probably testify to the fact that the most incredible and inspirational part of this book is that it was even written at all! For me to cheat my entire way through high school and bomb out of college miserably, this book is quite an accomplishment. For a gangster rapper who couldn't even spell half the words that I would use in my lyrics; writing a book is what some religions would call miraculous. You guys don't understand—I've never worked an hourly job that paid more than $10/hour. I've never been the best at ANYTHING I've ever been a part of. I wanted to play in the NBA, but I was too short for the position that I was good at in high school. I wanted to work for an airline as a flight attendant so I could travel the world and get paid for it, but they said I was too tall. I've always been a fan of R&B music, so I would sing my heart out in my bedroom every night trying to work on my vocals, but my voice never got any better. My dad said practice makes perfect and that anything I decided to work on I'd get better at. I practiced in my room for years, trying to sound like Slim from 112 or Sisqo from Dru Hill, but this was the one time I can remember my father being wrong. Can you imagine being too lame to be cool, but hanging around just enough cool and popular kids to not be considered all the way lame? Can you imagine being a gangster rapper but not really fitting in with the thugs because I always had a heart and a conscience that wouldn't allow me to do the really gangster activities? Can you imagine having insecurities that no one knows about, not even your best friends? Even now, I am considered a motivational speaker, but I still struggle with putting PowerPoints together. Because of how little attention I paid in grade school, I have a very difficult time organizing my thoughts and outlining what is on my mind and in my heart. So for today, finishing this book goes to show that no matter where you are on the timeline of your life, you can totally change the end of the story. Where you are has nothing to do with where you're going.

Jesus was a King, even though He was a carpenter. Did He become a King after He was a carpenter? What about when Jesus was a child? He was not yet a carpenter, meaning He definitely hadn't gotten to King status yet, right? That's ridiculous. Jesus was a King since birth. He was a King as a carpenter. He was a King before He walked this earth, and He is a King right now. YOU are a King or Queen no matter what your job title says you are. You are who God called you to be, not the title that people use to address you. Whether or not you are enjoying the physical manifestation of it yet, you are royalty. You ARE who you are going to be. It's already in you.

My biggest issue is that I thought I was who I was. I thought I was a college dropout who had a hard time understanding academics. I thought I was a hustler who would have to make money by manipulation because my brain couldn't wrap itself around the idea of becoming qualified to have a corporate job, which I initially wanted to have. I didn't understand that that wasn't who I was—it was just where I was on my timeline. From my understanding of great movies and biblical stories, everyone who becomes great doesn't fit the description of greatness initially. The movie is more entertaining when the least likely character becomes the superhero. If the handsome and educated guy who drives the Porsche gets the girl in the end, it's not too exciting—it's expected. The story of David and Goliath wouldn't be as fascinating or inspirational if David were the same size, strength, and age as Goliath and wore the same amount of armor. If this were the case, when David killed Goliath, no one would say God had anything to do with it. People would look at David as the hero. If they thanked God at all, they would thank God for SENDING David instead of OPERATING THROUGH David, thus giving David all the glory.

I must admit that now I can see the future in my present. Because of where I came from, I understand that everything that happens to me today is for someone else to benefit from tomorrow. What I go through today is a part of my life's testimony that will set someone else free tomorrow, so I rarely get discouraged anymore. How could you complain about the trials that are making you great? Why complain about the pain of working out when it's that very pain that makes you stronger? Someone buys you a brand-new bed, but you're so upset at the fact that you have to put the bed together yourself that you sleep on the floor. I'm at a point where I rejoice over all my current hardships. The worse things get, the better the story will end.

If you're going through a really rough time right now, I want you to document it so you don't forget how you feel in the moment. I need you to be able to look a little girl or boy in the eye and explain how your situation was way worse than theirs, but you got through it. I thought I had a handicap with reading and writing that would prevent me from being successful until I met a man who only had one arm who was way more successful than me. I thought I wouldn't be able to succeed in reading and writing because I just barely graduated from high school and cheated my way through. I didn't learn much in school because of my attitude, so I thought it would be impossible for me to do anything academically—until I met a high school dropout who became a doctor. My prayer for you is that you become the story that shows people that with any handicap, you can be an overcomer. You can be freed from any drug addiction that has you in bondage. Show them that you have been clean for 40 years when you used to get high 3 times a day. Someone on any level of poverty can become wealthy, and the only reason you know is because you hit rock bottom. It's the stories that set people free, not the success. It's the stories that inspire and encourage. It's the stories, YOUR stories, that save people. Why else would the bible use so many stories? The entire book is stories within stories. Embrace your story. I'm here to tell you that God can take anyone, and I do mean ANYONE, from the darkness that life has to offer and usher them into the marvelous light. I pray that my story sets you free and shows you that your dream CAN be built overnight, as long as you are willing to lose sleep in order to live the dream you have dreamt.

CHAPTER EIGHTEEN

A Letter to Mom

Dreams Are Built Overnight
-David Shands

What's up, my dear? I'm currently on vacation in Mexico, and I've been thinking about you more than ever lately, so I decided to lock myself in the hotel room and tell you a few things that I've never told a soul. Before I begin, I must inform you that I've been studying you for over 30 years now, and I finally found the answer to a question that I've been wondering about for years. It took some time to discover because of the complexity of the situation, but I finally put all the pieces together. Growing up in your household, so many things just didn't make sense for some reason, and now I know why. I have conclusive evidence that you have been less than honest with my brother and me this whole time. I haven't told Doug yet because I'm not sure he can handle the fact that everything he has ever known about you is a lie. I felt a bit disappointed when I discovered your secret, not because of the secret itself but because you apparently felt that you needed to keep information from us instead of being up-front and honest. The jig is up—I know without a shadow of doubt that you are a SUPERHERO with all kinds of superpowers. Don't try to deny it with more lies to blanket your true identity, Mom. I put all the pieces together, and it all makes sense now! I am prepared to back up my assumption with concrete evidence.

    I never understood, for example, how you could have no money and often be between jobs with literally no income, but you never let us go hungry. I know we had food stamps in the beginning of the month, but by the end of the month it was pretty bad. I vividly remember going to the refrigerator one day and finding nothing but condiments and water. I double-checked all the cabinets and found nothing. I went outside to play, and by the time my childhood hunger set in, I came home to a full dinner spread. How, Mom? I know you didn't leave the house because you didn't have any gas money. I've only heard of something like this happening once before—in church, when the pastor talked about how Jesus turned 2 fish and 5 loaves into a buffet to feed a small town, and you essentially did the same thing for 16 years. Explain that. Explain how in the world you could ALWAYS tell when I was hiding something from you. How could you possible say exactly what I'm thinking, when I'm thinking it in real time? Well, Mom, I looked it up and I found that there's a word for it: telepathy. What really tipped it off was that one day when I was watching the X-Men cartoon, I noticed that Professor X (also a superhero) had this same ability. I should have paid more attention to the signs, but I was too young and naive to think anything of it. THAT'S why you never really wanted us to watch TV or have our minds consumed by too many cartoons. This whole time I thought you would rather that I read or go out and play so I wouldn't become a lazy bum, but you just didn't want me to discover traces of your secret through cartoons. You ain't slick!

Also, it's very rare that I ever experience any type of depression, but on the days when I do, you always call me. How do you always know when I'm emotionally drained and need to talk? How could you possibly know that I'm in need of your encouraging words when I'm at my house and you're at yours? No mere human could possibly know these things and randomly decide to call with perfect timing. You gave away the fact that you could see the future a long time ago, and I should have paid attention. You've been telling me since I was a baby that I would own my own business, become extremely wealthy, and travel the world. Where did you get this information? No one in our family has ever done ANY of the things that you kept telling me I would, so what made you so sure? My entire grade school and college career was full of below-average achievements and failed classes. I've never had any superior ability in anything that show signs of future success, Mom. So HOW? How could you know that I would be doing what I'm doing right now? It would be different if you said things like, "I THINK you're going to be rich" or "I HOPE you become successful" or "You CAN change the world," but no—as sure as you are that the sky is blue, you told me about my future success with confidence and definitive statements. Why did you feel the need to tell me who I would become so often growing up? I always found it amazing and somewhat odd that you talked to me with such respect. You always spoke to me not like a kid but like a king. Even when you disciplined me, you did it with so much respect, only as necessary and never out of frustration.

What's it like having superpowers? I always wanted to ask Superman how it feels to know that he can leap tall buildings in a single bound and no one even knows about it. How does it feel to know that you have the power to turn a person's depression into joy with a simple hug and kiss on the cheek? What's it like knowing that you know what's best for me, even when I feel as though I have all the answers? A few times, I'm sure you wanted to say, "David, there's no point in going back and forth with me—I'm a superhero with superpowers; you're wrong and don't know it because you're just a human." However, that would have blown your cover, so you would instead say things like, "Well, I guess you'll have to learn the hard way, son." In a way, I'm glad you kept your identity a secret because I've become a better man by learning some things the hard way.

    I'm glad I got a chance to get all that off my chest through this letter. I really wanted to let you know that you mean the world to me. You've truly demonstrated what unconditional love is. Because of you, I understand love—not only what it is but also what it's not. Not a day has ever gone by when I was unsure about your love for me. Unfortunately, I must admit that I have taken your love for granted at times. I thought that the love you gave me was normal mother-son relationship love, but as I travel and interact with thousands of people across the world, I realize every day that there are levels to love. Not everyone has this divine connection that you and I share, and my heart genuinely breaks for those who have no idea what true love feels like. Your love for me has been so top tier that it's caused me to ruin a few really good relationships. I unintentionally used your love for me as a standard for how I should be loved by any woman who is in my life. I've made the mistake of thinking that the woman I'm with will love me the way you do. It's a very unfair standard for two obvious reasons: one, I know now that you're a freakin' superhero, and two, you've been learning about me and studying me for the past 30 years. There's no way I can expect a woman I just met to compare to our 30-year history. You know everything about me—my likes, my dislikes, and how I like my potato salad. You know when I need to be left alone, and you know when I need to be talked to. You have even learned how to tell me I'm wrong in a way that I'll receive well. These women have no idea who they're dealing with, and with that said, I'm going to do better in that area and get you those grandbabies you've been asking me about.

 In conclusion, Mother dearest, I would like to make you aware that you are responsible in many ways for the progression of my professional career. You told me once that you don't like when I tell people that my goal is to take care of you financially, because it makes you feel helpless, and because you have your own goals that you want to reach. You told me that you don't want people thinking that you're waiting on me to get rich so you can live off of me. You said you didn't like me telling people that we struggled financially, because it makes you feel as though you didn't take care of business as a parent. But you see, Mom, all of those experiences play in my mind when things get tough in my business. When I feel as if I want to give up, I realize that I wouldn't just be giving up on myself—I would also be giving up on the promises I made to myself for YOU. It would even be easy for me to break those promises if they were just between you and me because I'm sure you would understand. But I let it be known publicly because I want the world to hold me accountable. If I went and got my old job back at the Cheesecake Factory, and just made enough to live a comfortable life myself, I'd be a fraud. I can't stop now. I refuse to stop now. I teach kids all across the country that on their birthday, whether it's their 15th or 16th birthday, instead of asking for a gift that year, buy your parents a gift. Wash their car, clean the house—do something for your parents on

YOUR birthday. I teach them to keep an account of how long they have lived rent-free without paying any bills. If you lived for 16 years rent- and bill-free, you owe your parents at least 16 years of free rent. PERIOD! You are in debt for 16 years of rent, light, and water bill payments, and it's a debt that must be paid quickly. I tell them exactly what my vision is in regard to this payback plan, and Mom, you don't know it yet, but our story is inspiring thousands of people around the world. You are the battery in my back, and I love everything about you. You are MY superhero, my number one inspiration, and I am your biggest fan. I love you, Mom.

CHAPTER NINETEEN

Dreams Are Built Overnight
-David Shands

As we draw near to the ending of this book, I must admit that I have had a very clear advantage over 58% of young African American boys in America. My advantage was not something I did that made me extraordinary, but it was something that I had. What I had was simply by the grace of God and nothing that I was smart enough, diligent enough, or persistent enough to obtain. I was fortunate enough to have a man in my life long enough for me to become one. If you ever had a conversation with my father, you would understand how I consider my father a gift from God. He was so wise. Have you ever heard someone speak in riddles that you could understand? Every conversation I can remember challenged me to think. He rarely gave me the answers to the questions I asked, but he would always lead me to the answers, and in the end I would have to choose the answer myself. I thought that was pure genius. For example, I asked him one time, "Why do you always have people in our living room talking about business so late at night?"

He said, "You like to eat, don't you?"

It seems as though he answered ALL my questions like that. I know that wasn't all that deep, but as a child growing up, not getting clear-cut answers forced me to think critically if I wanted an answer. I began to equate business, late hours, and networking with providing for a family. If I wanted to "eat," I would have to do these things. It's hard to explain how we talked, so let me just call him on 3-way real quick. This is a long-distance call, so I'll make it brief. Hold on one moment...

Ring *Ring* *Ring* *Ring*

Pop: Hello?

Me: What's up, Dad? I was just talking about you. I just called to tell you a few things and ask you a few questions. Do you have a moment to talk?

Pop: Of course. Why wouldn't I make time for you?

Me: That's why I love you, Dad. How have you been?

Pop: If I had your hand, I'd throw mine in.

Me: You've been saying that for years. I never knew what it meant, but whatever; it must be some old-people slang. I was telling my friends about you, and I was trying to explain your parenting style. I remember you would have me dribbling up and down the street with only my left hand. Growing up, you always seemed to focus on my weaknesses instead of my strengths. I brought home a report card with 2 A's on it, and you said nothing about it, but we had an hour-long conversation about the D I got in science.

Pop: Why wouldn't you want to work on your weaknesses, son? I'm not interested in praising you all the time for what you're good at. What you're good at, you'll probably continue to be good at, but what makes you great is developing an above-average skill set at what you were previously bad at. What would happen if you became good at what you were bad at and slowly became better at what you were already good at? Being good in more than one area in the same field is what creates greatness. Michael Jordan wasn't the best rebounder, he wasn't the best passer, he wasn't the best 3-point shooter, he wasn't the strongest, and he wasn't the quickest player in the league. There were better free throw shooters in the league and also better defenders, but he was really good at everything, which made him what?

Me: Great?

Pop: Better than everyone else.

Me: So you'd rather I be good at everything than the best at something? That's strange—that would make me a jack-of-all-trades and a master of none...right?

Pop: Only if you are trying to be a good photographer, and a good web designer, and a good salesman, and a good rapper, and a good barber all at the same time. That's called stupid. A better option would be to develop ALL your attributes as a basketball player, or ALL your attributes in the field of photography, or ALL your attributes in the field of being a barber. What makes a GREAT photographer is that he develops ALL the various attributes of a photographer. He can shoot in studio light, natural light, club settings, anything. He can shoot indoors and outdoors. He can find the beauty in any environment. He can edit his pics, he can coach the model on how to pose, and so on. Now, I'm not saying anything is wrong with being the best 3-point shooter in the league, because that makes you great. Reggie Miller and Ray Allen are great, but it doesn't make you Mike...which is legendary.

Me: That makes sense. I didn't really call to hear another one of your sermons; I really wanted to tell you that I was thinking about you. I was thinking about the fact that you never disciplined me out of anger. I found it strange that we would have these little talks before you would beat me. While you were talking to me about how my misbehavior made you feel, I was honestly hoping that you would just get the whooping out of the way so we could get it over with.

Pop: It's not the flowers that get your point across; it's the little card that comes with the flowers that expresses why the flowers came.

Me: Huh?

Pop: The beating alone would be just a gesture of discipline, and it would be easy for you to think that I was mad at you. My goal was to inform you that I could never be mad at you—I was just mad at what you did. I never wanted you to confuse my hatred for your action with hatred for you. Did you ever hate me after a beating?

Me: Now that I think about it, no. Sometimes I wish you would have just beat me and gotten it over with because I began to get upset at myself for letting you down. It really helped me adjust my behavior and think about how it would make you feel if I did something dumb. You're a genius.

Pop: No, my goal was to be an example.

Me: The way you died, Dad, was very hard for me. You never let the doctors do an X-ray to find out what was wrong. You never even let them check. I know you preached to me that the body is designed to heal itself, and you pushed the message of good health, but come on, Dad, you were in hospice on your deathbed. Why not just let them check you out?

Pop: Where do you think you got your stubbornness from, David? I am a very stubborn man, and once I make up my mind, it doesn't change. Your whole life, I told you the dangers of these doctors who manufacture pills to cure one thing but to deteriorate something else. I told you that your body is a temple and you should treat it as such. You've never seen me take any prescription drugs or even get a checkup at a doctors' office, have you? I lived my life exactly how I told others to, and for the majority of your life, until my death, obviously I was very healthy. What kind of man would I be to tell you what I believe, but at the point of death, change my beliefs and compromise my lifelong message to save my own life. It may not make sense to you, but I believed what I believed, and no circumstances could change that. I would rather die for my beliefs than to live as a fraud. It's like as long as everything was good and Jesus was performing miracles, the disciples were die-hard Jesus fans claiming they would die for Christ. But as soon as things got a little tough and public opinion became important, Peter denied him, saying, "Jesus who? I never followed that guy." I'm not comparing myself to Jesus or anything, but I want to tell you that I died for you, my son. I died to show you that if you believe what you believe, you should be willing to die for that belief. We don't compromise our beliefs for convenience in this family, and just as a warning, there will come a time when you will be afforded an option to sell out. I don't know if someone will proposition you to make money by compromising your integrity, or if you will have a chance to win, but it will mean that one of your loved ones or friends will have to lose. I'm not sure what it will be, but I wanted to show you that a real man stands on what he believes in his heart is right, even if it means death.

Me: I would never compromise my integrity for public opinion.

Pop: Peter said the same thing, son.

Me: I guess I'll have to prove it one day, huh?

Pop: Sooner than you think.

Me: Thanks for taking the time to talk to me, Dad. I really miss you, and I thank God for you showing Doug and me how to be men. Doug is doing very well, by the way; he has a great career and a beautiful family. We don't fight or hate each other like we use to, and ironically he's actually one of my best friends. We don't talk as often as I'm sure you'd like us to, but when we do, it's all love and encouragement. We're both grown men, and even though it's not cool in 2015, when I see him I still give him a kiss on the cheek. It makes him uncomfortable, but who cares—I'm bigger than him now, so I don't think he can beat me up anymore.

Pop: I love you boys. Tell him I said hello and that I love him so much.

Me: Will do, Pop. I want you to know that I always remember to work as if you're watching me. I used to show out in my basketball games when I saw you in the crowd. I was very cognizant to go to my left to show you that those left-handed drills you had me doing were working. I never slacked on defense when I saw you watching because I knew that if I won the game with half effort, you would be upset, and if I lost the game but you saw me leave it all on the floor and play my heart out, you would let me rent a video game that night. I must say that it's been a pleasure growing up in your household. Thank you for being around. Thank you for being an example. Thank you for teaching me about hard work and sacrifice. Thank you for your tough love. Thank you for respecting my mother. Thank you for providing as a real man should. Thank you! Thank you! Thank you! I'll call you later when I finish crying.

Pop: Good night, son.

Wayne Steven Shands

(November 13, 1945 – November 21, 2010)

Bonus Chapter
"Strictly 4 Students"

Warning: This chapter may be very offensive to some adults, however, It doesn't really matter because it wasn't written for them anyway.

Dreams Are Built Overnight
-David Shands

As I stated earlier, my passion lies with mentoring and teaching our youth to think like an entrepreneur. I would be an absolute fraud if I didn't at least give you guys your own chapter to feast on! You all are my heart and a huge reason I continue to do what I do. Allow me to give you my perspective on formal education—yes, education! Despite my love for entrepreneurship, education is very important and essential to your success. I skipped kindergarten because of my education level as a child. My father did not wait to enroll me in school to begin my learning process, so by the time I got to kindergarten, I was so advanced that after a few months into it, I was promoted to 1st grade. Now, the fact that I got held back in 9th grade had everything to do with my lack of regard for education as a teenager, and I don't want you to make the same mistake.

Back in the day, my grandma used to tell me, "You need to get your education!" Now, what my grandma meant by that was, "You need to go to college"; she associated education in its purest form with going to college. She was so proud to see me in college at Alabama A&M University that she would tell people, "My grandson is in Alabama getting his EDUCATION." This statement couldn't be any further from the truth! I was in Alabama getting everything BUT an education! I was getting drunk, getting high, getting girls, and getting into trouble, but without seeing my grades, she told everyone that I was "getting an education." I actually went to 3 different colleges for an accumulated 6 semesters, and I am technically still a freshman, but as long as I was enrolled in a university, my family had hope that I was going to make it. I am not 100% sure as to what exactly they thought I was going to "make," or what "it" was, but for some reason they had hope. Whatever the case, no one ever sat me down and explained the purpose of learning a bunch of seemingly irrelevant information that I was sure I would never use. Do you want to know how I knew that I would never use this stuff? Because my parents could never really help me with my homework, and they could never help me with my homework because they did not know the answers, and they did not know the answers even though they learned those subjects at one point, because THEY HAVEN'T HAD TO KNOW THE ANSWERS SINCE THEY WERE MY AGE! It was so frustrating learning the Pythagorean theorem, how letters equal numbers, and that there is another little number that is much more powerful than the big numbers! "MAN, I am going to be playing basketball in the NBA, and if I don't, I'm going to be a big business owner or a rapper. You can keep all the letters—I just need to know how to count these millions I'm going to be making" were the recurring thoughts in my head at that age. In the mind of a 13-year-old kid, this thinking was completely logical. I wish someone would have sat me down and explained to me that school is just a game to play.

After about 5th grade, I started to realize that I hated school. I hated school and everything that it represented. I hated the fact that school seemed to be a fashion show, and because I was on the bottom of the totem pole in that department, I hated it. I hated that the girls only seemed to like the tough guys or the popular guys, and since I was neither tough nor popular, I hated it. Lastly, as I stated earlier, the seeming uselessness of the information being taught irked me to no end.

Thank God now for my frustration as a child, as well as my understanding now as an adult that school is simply a game.

I teach young men and women across the country that whether or not you think the information being taught in school is useful, school is just a game. The objective of any game you play is to win, and successful people play to win. I compare school to a game because thinking back to when I was in school that is pretty much all that interested me…GAMES. I have always enjoyed games because you have winners and losers. There are rules and regulations in every game, along with clear instructions on how to win. If I scored more points than the other team in the allotted time period, I would win. If I could avoid getting hit by the ball in dodge ball, I would win, or if I could hide so well that I couldn't be found for a long enough period of time (or, in certain cases, if the right girl found me while I was hiding), I would still win. I absolutely LOVED games, but I hated school; however, if I had thought of school as a game, I suppose I would not have hated it so much.

I tell kids that the way you beat this game is to get the grades by any means necessary. Like getting coins in Super Mario or any other game (I haven't been into video games since the '90s, so excuse me for this dated game reference), you have to obtain as many good grades as possible. It's not about simply moving up a level—it's about racking up as many coins (good grades) as possible, and here's why. For some reason, I noticed that teachers gave preferential treatment to the so-called "smart kids," or the kids with the most coins. If they came in a little late, not only would they not get in trouble, but sometimes teachers would act as though they didn't even see those kids come in late. I remember being in class talking to my "smart" friend Mike about something not pertaining to class during my teacher's lesson. When Mrs. Bardalas turned around and saw what was happening, judging by the frustration in her eyes, I knew we were in trouble (I was in trouble so much that I could recognize it before it even happened by this point in my middle school career). Now, I accept 50% responsibility for disrupting the class, so I was prepared to take my punishment like a man, even though I was only 11 years old. Mrs. Bardalas and I locked eyes, and at that point I knew it was going down, but what she said next SHOCKED me! She dropped the chalk, crossed her arms, and with a graceful ugliness shouted, "DAVID, you've interrupted this class enough! Go to the principal's office and tell him I sent you!" Now, I had been to the principal's office before, I knew all the secretaries by name, and they all knew me, so I was somewhat used to this part of my life; but the fact that she saw BOTH of us talking and said nothing to Mike opened my eyes to new truth. She only yelled at me as if I were some kind of weirdo who was talking to myself in class. Now, I couldn't say, "Mike was talking, too," because that would mean I was snitching, but I was heated for the rest of the day. In fact, if I remember correctly, Mike actually initiated the conversation that got me in trouble, so I was even mad at him for a couple of hours until he picked me to play on his team at recess; then we were cool again. Now, as an adult, I realize that Mike just had more coins than me, but as a child I never made the connection.

who people expect you to be. If you are generally a troublemaker and they see a disruptive crowd, if you're anywhere in the vicinity, they would assume that YOU probably had something to do with it. Because of my poor grades and lack of ambition to improve them even on days when I came in with a new desire to apply myself, my teachers would take my interest as sarcasm because in their eyes I was not that kind of student. If I asked a bunch of questions in order to understand a subject that I actually found interesting they would think I was being condescending and intentionally disruptive because of my track record. I was losing the game, and once you begin losing, it is hard to get people to take you seriously or even get them to look at you as a winner. I have found this principle to also be true in the job and career arena.

The way people perceive you is not the reward for winning the game. It lets you know you are on the right track, but that's not the sign that you have won the game. Most games that I am accustomed to playing have a number system at the end that tells you whether you have won or lost. Here is the ENTIRE reason that I decided to write this final section of the book: I believe that winning the game of school is achieved when you get to move up to the next level and you don't have to pay for it. That's it. That's how you beat the game.

What the game says is, "We (the game) will teach you to be a loyal, educated, and a stand-up citizen in the community for free, because if you have at least a basic education, you can help push our country forward. The country is built on the backs of high school graduates just like you who never furthered their education. All we (the game) will need you to do is get your high school diploma, which you will not have to pay for. That is our gift to you. In return, you will qualify to make an average of $31,000 per year as an entry-level employee, and within 10 to 20 years, studies show you will cap out at around $43,000 per year, almost 20% of which you will end up paying back to the government in taxes. Now, if you choose to, we (the game) will allow you to further your education, but it will be somewhat of a gamble. If you would be willing to take a loan from us, we will give you an average of $30,000 for more schooling. After completion, we will give you a sheet of paper (a degree) that will qualify you to walk into the workforce with an average entry-level salary of $46,000 per year. Now, you may or may not find a job paying that salary, and the experience you gained at your retail position working at the mall for the last 4 years while you were in college may possibly outweigh your degree when it comes to the workforce, but you will still have to pay back that $30,000 with interest, my friend. You can always do more schooling so you can come out making more money (which you will also have to pay back), but that is totally up to you. Now, we are willing to educate you for FREE, but it is based on how well you do with the FREE education we gave you in high school. Now, let's see your coins! If you have enough coins (good grades), we will end up not only paying for you to obtain this degree, but we will also pay you some extra money (scholarships) to live off of while you get through this training. At this point, whether or not you get a job after college, you will have the education that will allow you to walk into the workforce and earn money that we won't ask you for a piece of. You won't be bound by any debt like those coinless high school classmates of yours."

—Sincerely, The Game

So in conclusion, obtaining a degree without having to pay for it is how you win the game. Let's play ball!

Lessons Learned

Lessons Learned

REFERENCES

1. Buffet, Warren. AZ Quotes. Web. 1 Feb. 2015.
2. Kishore, Joseph. "Wealth of World's Billionaires: $7.3 Trillion." World Socialite Web Site. N.p., 19 Sept. 2014. Web. 26 Oct. 2015.
3. The Holy Bible, New Living Translation. Grand Rapids: Zondervan House, 1984. Print.
4. Carnegie, Dale. How to Win Friends and Influence People. New York: Simon and Schuster, 1981. Print.
5. "What's the Price Tag for a College Education?" COLLEGEdata. N.p., n.d. Web. 26 Oct. 2015.
6. Gladwell, Malcolm. Outliers: The Story of Success. N.p.: n.p., n.d. Print.
7. Allee, John Gage. Webster's Dictionary. New York: Galahad, 1975. Print.
8. Desmond, Adrian J. "Charles Darwin | Biography - British Naturalist." Encyclopedia Britannica Online. Encyclopedia Britannica, 21 May 2015. Web. 08 Nov.2015.<http://www.britannica.com/biography/Charles-Darwin>.
9. Admin. "Percent of Released Prisoners Returning to Incarceration." Crime in AmericaNet. N.p., 29 Sept. 2010. Web. 08 Nov. 2015. <http://www.crimeinamerica.net/2010/09/29/percent-of-released-prisoners-returning-to-incarceration/>.

10. "Girl Scouts | Official Web Site." Girl Scouts | Official Web Site. N.p., 2015. Web. 10 Nov. 2015. <http://www.girlscouts.org/>.
11. "The Extent of Fatherlessness." National Center for Fathering. N.p., n.d. Web. 10 Nov. 2015. <http://www.fathers.com/statistics-and-research/the-extent-of-fatherlessness/>.
12. Williams, Carolyn. "The Average Salary Without a College Degree." Work. N.p., n.d. Web. 10 Nov. 2015. <http://work.chron.com/average-salary-college-degree-1861.html>.
13. Rohn, E. James. 7 Strategies for Wealth & Happiness: Power Ideas from America's Foremost Business Philosopher. Rocklin, CA: Prima Pub., 1996. Print.